GENESIS:
Spirituality in Recovery from Childhood Traumas

Julie D. Bowden
Herbert L. Gravitz

 Health Communications, Inc.
Deerfield Beach, Florida

Library of Congress Cataloging-in-Publication Data

Bowden, Julie D. 1944-
    Genesis. Spirituality in recovery/Julie D. Bowden and Herbert L.
Gravitz.
        p.   cm.
    Bibliography: p.
    ISBN 0-932194-56-7 : $7.95
    1. Adult children of alcoholics — Psychology. 2. Adult children
of alcoholics — Religious life.   I. Gravitz, Herbert L., 1942-
    II. Title.
    HV5132.B68 1987   87-20572
    362.2'92 — dc 19   CIP

ISBN 0-932194-56-7

Published by Health Communications, Inc.
                Enterprise Center
                3201 SW 15th Street
                Deerfield Beach, FL 33442

Acknowledgments

We say a grateful "thank you" to all those who have had faith in this book and who patiently encouraged us through the halting process of preparation.

Special thanks to those early readers, Dr. Charles Whitfield, Rev. Denny Wayman, Dr. Peter Simeone, Rabbi Jonathan Kendall, Debbra Colman and Raymond Wilcove who brought us greater clarity.

Thanks also to the founding Board of Directors of the National Association for Children of Alcoholics. From the beginning, bonds were forged of a profoundly spiritual nature and those connections continue to teach us and nourish us. Also we send deep appreciation to Bill and Lois W., who brought the Higher Power into the healing of alcoholism. It is that same spiritual energy which today fuels the children of alcoholics movement.

And "thank you" to the editor, Marie Stilkind, who had faith in the importance of this book, working beyond the "call of duty" to prepare it for publication.

Dedication

This book is dedicated to all children of alcoholics and children of trauma who have been willing to touch their own secret pain in order to know healing and purpose, and to those who have allowed us to share in that most precious time.

Julie's Dedication

With love and gratitude for every teacher who has helped me on my way, especially the three souls who came as my children, Dondra Rae, Reyes Anthony and Danae Diane, who continue to teach me great lessons in courage, humility and unconditional love.

Herb's Dedication

To my family of origin, Philip B. Gravitz and Sophie Korem Gravitz, for their gift of life and their gift of love, which has been a continual source of security,

and

To my family of choice, Leslie Wilcove Gravitz, wife and soulmate, for her love and continual unselfish support, and my sons, Brian Eric, Aaron David and Jason Michael, who are the next generation.

Contents

Prologue

One evening as a friend was getting ready for her evening run, she heard a voice say, "Don't run tonight. Run in the morning." She was startled. She didn't know if she had imagined it. She couldn't see anyone. Nevertheless, she decided to follow the voice and run in the morning. The next morning she wondered if she would "hear" anything again as she started her run. She didn't. She finished stretching, left the house, and began jogging through the city streets. Then the voice came again.

"Run with your eyes closed." She was startled again but tried to respond to the directive. She took several steps with her eyes closed, then opened them, and continued running. The voice repeated, "Run with your eyes closed!" And she tried. For the rest of the run she closed her eyes several times. The last time was for a distance of several blocks. By the time she returned to the front of her home, she was crying from the power of the experience. She sat down on the sidewalk in front of her house.

And then the voice came to her once again. "It isn't faith if there isn't darkness." And again, "If you trust me, I will never fail you." And a third time, "If you trust me, I will never leave you" (Keller, 1987).

Such is the journey we are about to describe. It does not make much rational sense. It is certainly not very logical. But it is heartwarming and it is full of hope. It offers a source of new-found strength, increased consciousness, deeper relationships and more love. These are the fruits of the journey.

And this journey belongs to everyone. It is the same journey for the frustrated mystic at the corner bar, the flower child in Haight Ashbury, the beggar in India or the Catholic in the confessional. It is the same journey for the alcoholic, the co-dependent and all the other children of trauma. It is the journey of the heart wending its way Home. We are all fellow travelers. The noble of all lands, all cultures, walk in the same light. Many are the paths; one is the truth.

Introduction

Guide to Recovery,* our first book, presents the six stages of recovery for adult children of alcoholics (Gravitz & Bowden, 1985). Much has been happening in our country since we first described the "recovery continuum" in *Guide*. A shift in consciousness is reverberating across the land. A new respect, a new honoring of our relationship with ourselves, others and the universe is emerging. And a healing energy, a spiritual force, is finding its way into millions of homes as we find ourselves in the midst of a powerful social movement for adults who lost their childhood. Recovery is indeed occurring everywhere.

The National Association for Children of Alcoholics (NACoA) is now over 7,000 members strong. In February of 1987 NACoA began the process of forming state chapters as more and more people come together to spread its special message of hope to children of alcoholics of all ages. There is even CACoA, the Canadian Association for Children of Alcoholics.

---

*Redistributed by Simon & Schuster under the new title *Recovery,* 1987.

As we have presented recovery seminars around the country, we have continued to learn. While there is joy and hope as children of alcoholics learn to accept the legacy of their past, we have discovered that recovery, like life, is often difficult. Recovery requires knowing much of ourselves — and sometimes we would rather not know. Recovery requires that we see with different eyes, hear with different ears and acknowledge powerful, buried feelings. Recovery requires a new responsibility for ourselves. And as each stage of recovery evolves, so too does our consciousness. Becoming whole again requires a journey into and through the darkness of the wounds of childhood and healing the child within.

We have also come to appreciate how many of our wounds are spiritual. The price for survival can be a separation from our very soul, as well as a battered body or mind. More and more we have come to recognize our spiritual wounding and the importance of spiritual healing.

As we have talked to people throughout the country about the stages of recovery, we have noted a wide variety of feelings and responses to spiritual recovery. They are all very natural, very normal and very human, given our unique and special histories. They include relief, hope, joy, frustration, anger and even rage.

Relief, for example, may come to those of you who have known there is a spiritual component to the Children of Alcoholic's movement and your own recovery, but have not yet had your awareness validated. You know what it took to get as far as you have. Hope can derive from knowing that others are traveling the same road. The shock of recognition may come to those of you who have entered into this stage of recovery or are about to enter it, yet have not known what it was you were feeling. The joy, of course, comes from feeling yourself in harmony with the universe, and knowing you do not travel alone. What a difference that can make!

Frustration may come to those who want to leap-frog over the recovery process and get right to this stage, but still have other work ahead of you in the earlier stages. You want to get on with it now!

Anger may come to those of you who feel you have lost (or, more accurately, misplaced) your connection with your spiritual self along the way or feel as though you were betrayed in childhood by more than your parents. And you may also be angry or enraged at reading about the importance of spirituality in recovery. You don't want to trust again. Recovery demands spending time with many feelings, including anger at the prime force of the universe. Anger at God may be as necessary to experience as anger at our parents, drunk or sober. The important thing to know is the anger won't stay frozen if we allow ourselves to feel it. The only feelings that stay locked inside us are those we refuse to acknowledge.

We believe your feelings fit your experience at this moment and make sense, given what you have been through. And we believe that you are reading this at the right time to receive what you need. Some of you are reading this book because you read our first book, and you have chosen to continue the journey of recovery. Some of you are reading this book because you know or sense the importance of spirituality in your recovery. And some of you may not even know consciously all the reasons that bring you to these pages. It may be a "coincidence". Yet consider what author and psychiatrist Jerry Jampolsky says, "A coincidence is a miracle in which God chooses to remain anonymous" (1984).

Finally, we have come to believe that the stages of recovery for adult children of alcoholics (ACoAs) can also provide a blueprint of recovery for other adult children of trauma (CoTs) and co-dependents as well (Gravitz & Bowden, 1987).

Stages of Recovery

1. Survival
2. Emergent Awareness
3. Core Issues
4. Transformation
5. Integration
6. Genesis

Recovery begins with the survival of childhood. In the first stage called **Survival**, there may or may not be an awareness of God. Even when there is, underneath lies a barrier of unexplored childhood pain which causes you to stumble on your walk with God. Growing up in an atmosphere of unpredictability, arbitrariness, inconsistency and chaos, children learn what they are taught. And their primary teachers suffer from a disease of the mind, body and spirit. Life in this environment is emotionally damaging at best and, at worst, is terror-filled and dangerous. To survive in this atmosphere, children learn roles to adjust to a situation where they are neither seen nor accepted for whom they are. They grow up in a family of denial, where they are not free to voice what is in their heart and mind. They are not free to hear or trust that "still, quiet voice inside".

Some of you had an early, powerful relationship with God, but found God did not answer your prayers. You may have felt abandoned, not only by your parents, but by God as well.

One woman we worked with described how she negotiated with God. She told God that she would do all her homework on time, would not talk back to either parent and would help with the dishes every night without complaint if only God would make her father come home on time and her mother happy. She reported that she did her part but with no improvement in the situation. In fact at the end of that week, her father stayed out all night. When he got home the next day, her parents had a terrible fight. She stopped talking to God.

ACoAs and CoTs also turn from God because of apparent hypocrisy. At church, synagogue or temple everyone smiles and acts polite while no one seems to notice that there is something wrong. The ABC movie *"Shattered Spirits"* showed a dinner scene with the family saying Grace before the meal, followed immediately by a bitter confrontation between the alcoholic father and the son. So in survival, even if spirituality is part of your life, the old unexplored, unacknowledged pain will assert itself. You find yourself acting in ways that do not make sense, or doing things you wish you had not done.

In the second stage called **Emergent Awareness**, spirituality makes its appearance in what we term the "first awakening". In Emergent Awareness, ACoAs and CoTs experience hope that something can change their life and actually make it better. This is born of faith in something greater than yourself, in a Higher Power, be it God, a fellowship or a book. The individual has reached a place of despair or desperation which results in surrender to an outside source of help. It may only appear as a slender thread at first. From that surrender there is a commitment made to your own recovery. Here connections are made between the present and the past. Current suffering takes on meaning. You begin to realize that your feelings of low self-esteem and inability to experience intimacy or satisfaction result not because you are bad, sick, crazy or dumb, but because you learned dysfunctional patterns in childhood. This might be the first time you have considered that it was something outside you that caused you to feel so badly. It might be your first hint that there is nothing inherently wrong with you, that you were not born damaged.

Once these connections are made, the third stage begins. In **Core Issues** children of alcoholics or other trauma learn the identity of their chronic stumbling blocks. The energy from the hope in Emergent Awareness and the knowledge in Core Issues make the passage to the next stage of recovery possible. However, it is here that recovery stops if you are chemically dependent. No further progress can occur. Even your current walk with your spiritual self is impaired if you are chemically impaired. That inner guidance can not be found through a chemical fog.

Once we learn to call a thing by its right name, **Transformation**, the fourth stage, follows. New ways of living, thinking and acting are learned. The old ways are seen for what they are — outmoded, archaic relics from a hostile environment which no longer serve in this new world. After these lessons are learned, the ACoA and CoT has learned to dance a new dance and to relate in a new way to self and others.

From this transformed and empowered position the fifth stage of recovery emerges. This stage, called **Integration,** is a consolidation of the new behaviors, and is a congruence among thoughts, feelings and actions. Here is where what you are thinking relates to what you are feeling and your actions are an expression of both. This is the stage in which some children of alcoholics choose to remain.

And sometimes there evolves a sixth or spiritual stage of recovery for wholeness which also leads to holiness. This last stage, which becomes the beginning of a qualitatively new life and a new commitment, is called **Genesis**. It is the next step of the journey.

There are many ways to approach Genesis. We believe it is viewed and experienced differently by each person. Just as each person's view of the world is colored by his or her own personal history so, too, each person's view and experience of spiritual aspects of life are unique. There is no one right way to perceive spirituality, no one right way to live in the stage of recovery we call Genesis. Again the truth is one but the paths are many. Given the variety of needs and perspectives among adult children, we suggest you accept what fits for you and leave what does not.

Regardless of what brought you to these pages, hello and welcome! Thank you for joining us on this leg of the journey. Settle back and relax as you read what follows. Keep an open mind. Take nothing for gospel. Taste everything and swallow only what nourishes you. You have just taken one more step in your recovery.

1

What Is Genesis?

Our normal waking consciousness, rational consciousness as we call it, is but one special type of consciousness, whilst all about it, parted from it by the filmiest of screens, there lie potential forms of consciousness entirely different. We may go through life without suspecting their existence, but apply the requisite stimulus, and at a touch they are there in all their completeness . . . No account of the universe in its totality can be final which leaves these other forms of consciousness quite disregarded (James, 1902).

The Essence and History of Being Human

All forms of life manifest a powerful tendency to grow, to unfold and to move toward fulfillment. This desire for expansion is a part of the very nature of life itself; it is at the basis of all progress. Contemporary psychology has observed and described this tendency toward fulfillment. As psychologist Carl Rogers stated, there is an ". . . actualizing

1

tendency which is present in every living organism — the tendency to grow, to develop, to realize its full potential" (1985).

This psychology of fulfillment or the "transpersonal movement" was anticipated by Abraham Maslow (1962), one of the founders of humanistic psychology. His theory of a hierarchy of needs started with basic physiological needs, such as food and shelter, then moved through safety, belonging, self-esteem, and was thought to end with self-actualization. The idea of "higher consciousness" was so controversial that Maslow hesitated until late in his life to reveal "transcendence," the last stage of his "recovery continuum" (1971). The cautiously added transcendence need was spirituality. Psychiatrist Carl Jung posited the existence of a *collective unconscious* to which all humans have access (1965).

Philosophy, theology, mysticism and even modern science, all point to a comprehensive awareness that reaches beyond or transcends ordinary, every day states of consciousness. This comprehensive awareness lies beyond what we can experience through our unaided physical senses (Whitfield, 1985; Capra, 1982).

Many people have reported altered states of consciousness wherein they have extraordinary experiences, e.g., deja vu, precognition, reverie. In fact, a 1985 Gallup poll found that 43% of all Americans report having had unusual spiritual experiences. Others have heard descriptions of a person exhibiting "superhuman" strength in a crisis, such as women lifting cars off a baby or men running to rescue a child faster than they could ever run under ordinary circumstances. These examples of abilities and resources, which go beyond the ordinary or the expected hint at a reality that is more than what we normally perceive.

Throughout history, as well as recent scientific literature, ways have been described to reach higher levels of mind or altered states of consciousness, well-being and health. Common to such seemingly diverse perspectives is a vastly more expansive view of our relationship to a universal power or source.

According to Whitfield (1985), the two most striking features of this view are that:

1. A part of the universal Higher Power or God exists in the consciousness of each human being.
2. Consciousness exists as a hierarchy of dimensional levels, moving from the lowest, densest and most fragmentary realms to the highest, subtlest and most unitary ones.

Words Are Inadequate

This dimension of expanded consciousness, this spiritual dimension, is the essence of the stage of recovery we call Genesis. Its presence was confirmed to us and made manifest on Valentine's Day, 1983, in the founding of the National Association for Children of Alcoholics (NACoA). People of healing from across the country came together and made a commitment outside of and beyond themselves, and they bore witness to a social movement of immense proportions. Many of the founding board members described NACoA as a "coming home". For others it has become a source of hope. For all there was an end to the silence.

Genesis is a far more difficult stage of recovery to describe than those we have discussed previously (Gravitz & Bowden, 1985). Paraphrasing T.S. Eliot, Genesis is the end that becomes a beginning. What distinguishes Genesis is a new and varied relationship to self, to others, to the universe — to life.

Genesis supports, nourishes and maintains recovery. It casts a hallowed light over all stages of recovery. While Genesis is ever present, not everyone consciously experiences it, and no one experiences it in quite the same way as another.

One of our clients expressed it this way: "Without knowing very early that I wasn't alone — that there was a greater force — I could have never continued with my recovery." Another said, "Whenever I ran out of gas, there was that intangible bond connecting me with all that I was, all that I am and all that I could be." And another remarked that Genesis was "truly like coming home to a warm comfortable place."

PERVASIVE

As suggested, Genesis is another stage of recovery, yet manifests in each prior stage. For example, in Survival it tends to be all or nothing, either embraced totally, without the inclusion of the foundation from the earlier stages, or disowned and disavowed. In Emergent Awareness it provides a glimpse of a hopeful, new awakening, while in Core Issues it lends strength to the commitment, and in Transformation it fuels the change process. Integration manifests Genesis, but without conscious awareness.

Whereas Integration initiates a coherency and congruency among the thoughts, feelings and actions of adult children, there is a powerful expansion of body, mind and soul in Genesis. This is the hallmark. This is the paradigm shift. It is the difference, for example, between playing the piano with one finger or playing with ten. It is the difference between one instrument and the whole orchestra. The melody is qualitatively different. It is viewing life's meaning as greater than we can know with our limited senses of taste, touch, sound, sight and smell; yet Genesis includes these physical senses, too. Hence, it is a stage beyond integration, while embracing everything contained in previous stages.

THREE FACETS

In Genesis there is a personal, powerful, enduring relationship with God (or whatever term you use to refer to the higher power). It reveals itself in three primary ways: feelings, awareness and lifestyle.

Each person seems to emphasize a special area respectful of who they are. It is much like the many facets of yoga. One path is through wisdom, another through devotion, another through service, another through power and so on. Thus, some people understand Genesis more than they feel it. Another may not have a clear perception of Genesis, but incorporates activities into her or his lifestyle that honor the divine.

The feeling aspect of Genesis is the way it is emotionally experienced. The emotions of joy and peace develop as a person's awareness and lifestyle change toward a more loving existence.

The story of what happened to Bill W. in Towns Hospital during his last hospitalization for late-stage alcoholism is a wonderful example.

Bill had a profound spiritual awakening that included a vision that forever altered his life. During that vision he felt himself lifted to a hilltop. He felt the Presence of a great power and experienced peace and oneness with that power. Ever afterward, Bill felt assured of the existence of God.

The awareness aspect of Genesis is a way of understanding or knowing the world. It is seeing the world as full of meaning.

Genesis reveals heights of human awareness that enlarge and extend our view of reality. Awareness is elevated to states of consciousness where the multi-dimensional nature of existence is perceived and celebrated. Throughout most of our lives there are moments when we question the purpose of our existence. The stage of Genesis answers with the existence of a transcendent power. Genesis places our entire life's experience into a more meaningful perspective, and we move beyond the identity of child of an alcoholic to child of God. This is especially relevant for ACoAs and CoTs who have railed against God because of their traumatic history.

Several examples can help make this altered perspective of consciousness clearer. Marilyn Ferguson writes in *The Aquarian Conspiracy:*

> A mind unaware of itself — ordinary consciousness — is like a passenger strapped into an airplane seat, wearing blinders, ignorant of the nature of transportation, the dimension of the craft, its range, the flight plan and the proximity of passengers . . . The mind aware of itself (by contrast) is a pilot. True, it is sensitive to flight rules, affected by weather and dependent on navigation aids, but still vastly freer than the 'passenger' mind. This 'consciousness of consciousness' is sometimes referred to as a higher dimension. Like the passenger in the plane, we can remain blind. Our beliefs can limit us or set us free (1980).

Rigid belief systems limit us to living in ordinary consciousness only, much as knowing one language limits us to the concepts describable in only that language. Our everyday, fixed beliefs and ideas are conditioned by our history, culture, race and gender.

For example, Eskimos do not have just one word for snow but many words. They recognize snow in a multitude of forms, and have names for each. As a result, they *see, feel* and *hear* an expanded and multidimensional variety of snow.

Maharishi Mahesh Yogi, the founder of trancendental meditation, provides another analogy (1963). Imagine, he says, a person who has always lived in a completely darkened movie theater with nothing visible but the movie when it comes on the screen. Knowing only the movie, this person assumes his experience is determined by the events on the screen. There is no perspective of a larger context. When the projector is turned off, there is no experience. He is asleep. During the darkness he sometimes becomes dimly aware, creating illusory movies. He is dreaming. If he is able to leave the projector on, fade the image on the screen until the screen itself becomes visible, he can begin to realize the nature of the theater itself. He ultimately becomes so familiar with the theater that he sees the screen, even during the movie. Now he not only enjoys and understands the theater, but for the first time he can really enjoy the movie. The content of the film once dominated him. Now the properties of the projected image on the screen become a source of delight.

These analogies help reveal some of the limitations of our everyday awareness of reality and how this limited awareness affects our experience of the world. Our experience comes alive through our awareness. But awareness precedes and is independent of experience. Just as understanding the real nature of movies enhances a person's enjoyment of every movie, full knowledge of the self in expanded awareness provides a stable basis for moving beyond what has previously seemed apparent and increases the enjoyment of life.

It is still true that if you hit your head on the projector or the screen, it hurts. But if it is recognized as only a small part of a larger theater or world, the hurt captures less of our attention, like the difference between a small burn on the finger and a burn over 90% of the body.

As a lifestyle, Genesis would find a person taking time daily to honor his or her humanness, to appreciate the universe and to give and share with others. It is not necessary to have a clear awareness of God or to feel the presence of a higher power in your life. It is only necessary to live a life that expresses the best of being human. There is a conscious commitment to live a life of love.

In Genesis we are mindful of the values out of which we operate and make an effort to express our highest values. A story of Mahatma Gandhi tells of him boarding a train when a man rushed up to him pleading, "Give me a message to take back to my people!" Gandhi scribbled a message on a paper bag, tore it off and handed it to the man. It read, "My life is my message" (1957).

The Larger View

Genesis in its most basic sense enlarges our inner vision to apprehend the positive, the creative and the spiritual. It makes us aware of the entire reality behind our more limited, conscious experience. Much as the microscope and the telescope extend our vision to otherwise unknowable distances, Genesis uses the mind and heart to extend reality to include the spiritual realm.

Genesis illuminates all the shades of grey and hosts a continuum of spiritual experiences from the momentary and fleeting to the attainment of a boundless, inner field of pure universality, e.g., bliss, samadhi, nirvana. It is the pathway to potentially inexhaustible, positive energy that heals the pain of years of struggle, empowers the common and nourishes the whole being.

In Genesis the trauma of childhood is seen at last as the necessary pathway to the present. We witness the emergence of creativity forged from the wounding childhood. Richard Farson (1978) developed what he calls the "Calamity Theory" in which strength comes from coping with adversity, much as a broken bone becomes even stronger at the precise point of the fracture. Some immunization shots are actually small doses of the bacteria from which one is being protected. The body responds by building the desired antibodies, enabling the individual to combat future infections.

Thus Genesis is a metaphor for spirituality and takes many forms. It requires a commitment and faith much different from that required by the other stages of recovery. However, throughout the entire recovery process, we may take steps to heighten our awareness of universal consciousness. As this expanded awareness is developed, we become increasingly free to choose a "Genesis lifestyle". It is our action grounded in conscious contact with our spirituality that empowers us to become co-creators of our lives.

2

Is Genesis Only For Children Of Alcoholics?

For years it lay in an iron box buried so deep inside me that I was never sure just what it was. I knew I carried slippery, combustible things more secret than sex and more dangerous than any shadow or ghost. Ghosts had shape and name. What lay inside my iron box had none. Whatever lived inside me was so potent that words crumbled before they could describe. (Epstein, Children of the Holocaust, *1981).*

Children of Trauma

As we have traveled, presenting lectures and workshops on the recovery process for children of alcoholics, we have come upon another simple but powerful truth. In towns and cities throughout our country people have come to us saying, "I read your book and it really helped me, but I'm not the child of an alcoholic."

More and more people who were not children of
alcoholics began to tell us that the recovery process really
began to match their experience when they heard about the
"Core Issues". Then they would say, "You hit me right
between the eyes!"

So we contined to learn and we began seeing what many
of our colleagues were discovering as well: children of
alcoholics are but the visible tip of a much larger social
iceberg which casts an invisible shadow over perhaps 96%
of the population in this country. These are the Children of
Trauma (CoTs), the children of dysfunctional families.
Without diminishing the powerful pain of children of
alcoholics, we would like to validate the other children of
trauma who too are finding a road map of recovery in the
children of alcoholics' movement.

Surviving their childhoods, rather than experiencing
them, these children of trauma have had to surrender a part
of their very being, their very soul, to go on. Languishing in
adulthood, they perpetuate the denial and minimization
which encases them in dysfunctional roles, rules and
behaviors.

These are the children of our time, these children of
trauma. Over 200,000,000 of us denying our past, submerg-
ing our realities and ultimately misplacing both the "little"
self and the "big" self. Profound devastation in the midst of
chaos! Quite a legacy so many of us inherit from our parents
and pass on to our children.

Who are they? Who are these children of trauma? They are
the children raised in other kinds of troubled family
systems. Often CoTs are grandchildren of alcoholics. They
have been raised by an unrecovering adult child of an
alcoholic. Their parent exhibited all the core issues
themself, but like all ACoAs who live their lives out in the
stage of survival, they suffered without meaning. And often
the alcoholism of the previous generation was never
identified or never discussed. These adults indeed share a
similar history with children of alcoholics and can find help
and meaning in the recovery process.

Other CoTs are children who grow up under the influence of compulsive behaviors, such as eating disorders, workaholism, gambling, money, sex or even "loving too much". They are the children who grow up in families where there is neglect and abuse or there is mental or physical illness in which denial and misinformation fueled a fire of guilt and blame. They may have experienced life through the horrors of holocaust or genocide trauma. Some come from perfectionistic, judgmental or other non-loving families who appeared normal or well functioning on the surface. In all of these families rigidity prevents human unfoldment. In the name of love children are ignored, abandoned, isolated and abused. Visible as never before, child abuse is marring untold millions.

These children of trauma suffer physical damage, they suffer emotional damage and they suffer spiritual damage. There is a destruction of trust, an abandonment of self and the wisdom of their experience. And there is a loss of faith in the joy, hope and splendor of life. These children face their family's unique trauma and, indeed, develop characteristics similar to the child of an alcoholic.

These CoTs, like ACoAs, lived daily in families of trauma. The impact is devastating. An example of the power of only a brief time in a traumatic situation can perhaps help us appreciate the influence of such a childhood.

Held Hostage

In the 1970s a bus load of children was abducted in a California town called Chowchilla. The children were held hostage for less than a day before being rescued. Researchers discovered that five years later these children were still exhibiting symptoms of being traumatized. They felt stigmatized and expressed magical thinking. They were still trying to explain to themselves how they should have had power to influence the situation, such as one child who said he had seen a movie about kidnapping on television the night before and believed that had been a warning that he should have heeded (there was no such movie shown). Or the child who said she had seen some strangers in the store the day before and should have known. If only a few hours can produce such an impact, consider the impact of up to 18 years, every day living in a situation where you are not allowed to be who you are, or feel what you feel. There is an old saying that alcoholics don't have relationships, they just take hostages.

The common denominator for CoTs is that the child is unable to be who he or she truly is. She is asked to abandon herself. He is asked to not feel what he is feeling. And these core issues or key problems cannot be mentioned. Unmentionable becomes unmanageable. Unwritten rules dictate what is and what is not permissible or discussable.

CoTs learn what Claudia Black calls "a high tolerence for inappropriate behavior" (1985). They do not know what they know! Ignoring the obvious, they become enslaved by rigid roles and oppressive rules, and are often bound to inflict generational damage upon their own children. Ignoring their own inner experience of the world, they become estranged from themselves, the child within and their very soul.

These other survivors of childhood trauma are learning to recover too. And we have come to believe that the very same process that offers recovery to children of alcoholics produces recovery for children of trauma. Because not all children of trauma make it through childhood, their recovery begins with the survival of childhood.

Until recently, Survival was the only stage of recovery. That is changing. CoTs, like AcoAs, reach adulthood feeling sick, bad, crazy or dumb. They feel inherently flawed. Their Emergent Awareness is as powerful and liberating as the ACoAs and their Core Issues are the same. A Transformation can occur which leads to a life-enhancing Integration of the individual's disowned parts, and ultimately back to the spiritual connection which is the Genesis of a new life.

All Children of Trauma

Children of alcoholics are not apart or separate from the rest of humanity. The plight of children of alcoholics is a reflection of the very human predicament in which children of all ages can find themselves. Like other children of trauma they develop wounds in their spirit. Genesis is for the children of all people of all ages in all places and at all times. It complements and embraces recovery from all conditions human.

So, "Yes!" Genesis applies to all children of trauma — all individuals who suffered silently in childhood, becoming adults who are unable to appreciate their own uniqueness.

If you are all grown up on the outside but feel little on the inside, if you feel bad, sick, crazy or dumb, then this book may be of help to you, too. Welcome. We wish you well on the journey. This time it's your time to recover too.

3

Must I Go Through
The Stage Of Genesis?

*You are accepted . . . accepted by that which is
greater than you and the name of which you do
not know. Do not ask the name now, perhaps you
will know it later. Do not try to do anything,
perhaps later you will do much. Do not seek for
anything, do not perform anything, do not intend
anything. Simply accept the fact you are accepted
(Paul Tillich, 1950).*

Recovery Is Three-Fold

Recovery from the disease of alcoholism is threefold:
physical, emotional and spiritual. We believe no less is true
for children of alcoholics and other children of trauma. Just
as William James described alcoholics as "frustrated
mystics" (1902), we believe children of alcoholics are also
frustrated seekers of that ultimate, unbounded relationship
possible only on the spiritual level.

15

Many adult children seek that ultimate relationship with a drug or a mate, and they are disappointed time and again. So a restlessness may mark your relationships until you enter Genesis. You may find that sharing your time or your life with someone brings you a certain comfort, happiness or peace which "wears off" after a while. So you need a "fix" over and over. This may mean you change intimate relationships several times.

And even in Genesis, there is what has been called a "divine discontent" (Thomsen, 1975). After Bill W.'s "luminous instant of insight", the co-founder of Alcoholics Anonymous (AA), himself an alcoholic and the child of an alcoholic (Kurtz, 1979), worked daily on continuing to live what he had experienced in that moment with an increasing awareness that he was much more than his earthly identity. Years after his sobriety was attained, Bill wrote to a close friend:

> Last autumn depression, having no really rational cause at all, almost took me to the cleaners. I began to be scared that I was in for another long chronic spell . . . By the hour, I stared at the St. Francis prayer ' . . . it's better to comfort than be comforted.' Here was the formula . . . but why didn't it work? Suddenly I realized what the matter was. My basic flaw had always been dependence, almost absolute dependence, on people or circumstances to supply me with prestige, security and the like . . . Reinforced by what grace I could secure in prayer, I found I had to exert every ounce of will and action to cut off these faulty emotional dependencies upon people, upon AA, indeed any act by circumstance whatsoever. Then only could I be free to love . . . Emotional and instinctual satisfactions, I saw, were really the extra dividends of having love, offering love and expressing love . . . Nowadays, my brain no longer races compulsively, in either elation, grandiosity or depression. I have been given a quiet place in bright sunshine. (1953)

Faith and living in Genesis are as much a challenge as staying sober one more day. And although there are instances when a spiritual awakening comes in a flash, or drinking is stopped miraculously, such as occurred for Bill W., it seldom just happens. And even then, as Bill's letter indicates, our efforts are still required for growth to continue. If you *do* want to discover and experience this stage, it will take renewed energy and commitment.

Genesis is neither a mystery nor is it an impossible climb to turn one's energy to this higher stage of living. It begins with simply being aware of the possibilities, wanting to make the change, and then slowly, over time, developing a supportive lifestyle.

As the psychologist Erich Fromm stated, "The practice of faith and courage begins with the small details of daily life" (1974). Yet, like the delicate butterfly, a symbol of freedom and recovery as well as a metaphor for spirituality, if we try to grasp it, we will crush it. To experience, appreciate and enjoy it, we have to let it go. So even if you feel somewhat hesitant, you can still start, but start with a light step.

The Spiritual Separation

For many reasons, adult children of alcoholics or other children of trauma often have particular difficulty approaching Genesis. Early in childhood, these children are taught not to trust themselves. This early divorce from the self seems to include a wrenching separation from the "soul" or Higher Self. Trust is ruptured.

A classic example of this rupture is illustrated in the following dinner scene: Mom, Dad and child sit down to eat. The alcoholic (Dad in this case) has been drinking. He reaches for something on the table, loses his balance and tips over his chair. Over he tumbles onto the floor, hitting his head on the way down. He lands with a grunt. The child goes on red alert. A crisis is occurring. With blood racing, heart pounding and adrenalin flowing, the child is impelled to leap to her feet. Just as she does, a hand lands firmly on her shoulder. Mother's voice orders: "Sit down. Eat your dinner. Nothing's the matter." As Father struggles to get up, he says with a surly tone, "What's the matter with you? What are you staring at?" The child looks from one to the other. Her internal wisdom says something is wrong. Her parents say nothing is wrong. Whom can she believe? Neither? Her own eyes and ears?

The child has two choices. She can be right or she can be safe. She cannot be both! To be right is to believe her own internal sense of the world and challenge her parents saying, "Yes, there is something wrong. Dad fell down. I'm afraid he hurt himself and I'm scared." That would be right but not safe. She is likely to be contradicted, threatened or physically abused. To be safe is to sit down, to tell herself that her insides must be wrong and therefore can't be trusted as guides. To be safe is to pick up the fork and begin to eat, forcing food through the tightness in her throat and the knot in her stomach.

When a child's sense of reality is continually invalidated, he or she learns not to trust the people who contradict the internal messages. But even more devastating, the child learns not to trust her own internal sensory experience, and ultimately, the still, quiet voice inside. Many religions direct us to ". . . the kingdom within" for our connection to the spiritual dimension of life. Children of trauma learn in a thousand ways to ignore the messages from within, because the trauma continues and this scene is repeated over and over.

Then perhaps later that night that child goes to her room. As she lays down to sleep, she prays to Someone to help her and to help her mom and dad. The next morning, her father, feeling quite guilty, promises her an ice cream cone "date" after he returns from work. She is excited. Someone answered her prayers! All day she looks forward to the special time with Dad and eagerly awaits his homecoming. And waits. She finally gives up because Dad does not come home that night. And she concludes no one was listening to her prayers. Prayer only seems to invite false hope.

This early abandonment is graphically described in the following letter we received:

> I was forced to go to Sunday School by myself. My parents were too busy drinking to come with me. At church I was taught you don't drink, smoke or dance, otherwise you will burn in eternal hellfire. You folks got to be kidding me! Is God blind? Why doesn't he spend a night in my home? And please, God, close all the liquor stores. I guess God was deaf, too. He never answered the prayers that ended with that plea.

Another difficulty children of early trauma may have with Genesis is that the word "God" is often equated with the word "love " or with authority. Our first teachers of love are our parents. If the people who love us the most, hurt us the most, then love becomes a painful experience to be avoided. The abandonment and pain that occurs at the parent's hands is at some deep level also attributed to "the powers that be".

In an alcoholic home the parents become increasingly incapacitated. Children are forced to grow up quickly and often assume the role of parent to their parents. If these early authorities, our parents, are incompetent, untrustworthy or abusive, which they often are, children learn not to respect or trust authority. A Higher Power is obviously not going to find a ready home in this individual. The early separation from self and learning not to trust the inner self leaves the child of an alcoholic or other trauma with few resources to protect himself or herself. When the internal messages have been discounted for years, messages of intuition or the Higher Self, which are often discerned from within, may seem to be insanity, confusion or, at the least, suspect.

One client, an ex-nun, told of walking out of her home after a particularly ugly fight between her alcoholic parents. While kicking the tires of the family car, she looked upwards and cried, "If there is a God, you're mean and I hate you! " It is easy to understand her anger and loss of faith!

The question begs to be asked: "If there is a God, why is this happening to me?" Or, "What kind of God lets this happen?" Young children do not have mature thought processes. In fact, children are very egocentric, believing themselves to be at the center of everything. It is natural for children to assume that what is happening is a result of their own behavior. Even adults have difficulty understanding seeming tragedy.

We don't know all the "whys", but we do know many adult children who have made peace and sense out of their experience. From a spiritual vantage point, childhood — even one which is traumatic, perhaps especially one which is traumatic — is designed to serve a purpose. Awareness of this purpose in the early stages of recovery is typically absent, and can potentially inhibit the healing process by blocking the expression and experience of feelings. For instance, if we "understand" that our parents beat us because they, too, were beaten as children, it can cause us to feel guilty for feeling angry. After all, they did the best they could. In those caring stages we need to feel free to add the next thought ". . . and their best was not good." Awareness of this history and purpose in Genesis gives us the power to set a new course. It allows full forgiveness finally, and makes space for love.

Baba Hari Dass (1986), a respected spiritual teacher from India, describes the effects of living with an alcoholic parent this way:

> Children of alcoholic parents are deprived of love from their parents, and they see their parents in a different world so they feel lonely. They don't get any training about life in the world, so they don't find their limits on their actions, decisions, habits. Also we all inherit . . . tendencies from our parents. Some are good, some are bad. Where there is no one to guide us, support us and love us, then these tendencies start growing like a weed in a garden and cover up the discriminative mind. We need to remove the weed by learning disciplines of life.

The Message of Genesis

The message that Genesis holds is that we no longer need to accept a limited, unhappy reality and that there really is more to life than our senses perceive. There are different levels of creation, all present simultaneously, just waiting to be rediscovered. Lack of knowledge, awareness and commitment to this larger reality can be like a building without a foundation, a ship without a rudder, or a checkbook without funds.

Recovery encompassing Genesis is to live with sure and joyful knowledge that your recovery matters in a universal sense, beyond yourself. It is to live with awareness that the pebble dropped into the pond sends out ripples, indelibly affecting the water's surface. Each and every person's work of recovery is important not only for that individual, but also for the other lives it affects. Just as alcoholism is said to affect at least four other lives, so too do we believe each person's recovery affects at least four other lives. And the effects on these people is multiplied through the following genera- tions. Genesis is the stage where we can make a conscious decision that the effect we have on others is positive.

This concept of affecting others can be likened to a relay race. The work of each runner affects every other runner. Each runner on the team is integral and the combined work is consummated when the anchor person hits the tape at the finish line. Thus, some people believe that until all people are free, no one is free. In the early stages of recovery, this may be expressed as co-dependency, the feeling that we are responsible for others. In Genesis this sense of responsibil- ity to others is the awareness that we are all connected, we are all one. And while we are concerned for others in Genesis, we do not attempt to live their life for them.

Complements Recovery

Genesis complements the recovery process; it does not compete with it or supersede it. What seems increasingly

apparent to us is that the previous stages of recovery help
people to build a solid foundation of relationships, values
and skills. We are able to achieve *situational* happiness and
intermittent serenity. Genesis, on the other hand, leads to
foundational happiness and *inherent* serenity built on the
solidness of the foundational work of the earlier stages.

For some, Genesis may follow a period of time and
comfort. You do not have to rush into Genesis. So, you may
spend years working on the previous stages. And you
certainly do not have to explore Genesis, but you may want
to. One of the paradoxes of Genesis is that when the time is
right, you will naturally turn toward it; yet, you can also
actively seek that time.

It may be helpful in the beginning to keep in mind that if
it *is* true there is a higher power or God and you accept that
existence as part of your reality, you have everything to gain.
If it not true, you have nothing to lose.

As Bill W. said, "Do not let any prejudice you may have
against spiritual terms deter you from honestly asking
yourself what they might mean to you" (AA General Service,
1973).

This is perhaps a good point to stop reading and check
your reactions. Ask yourself how you were affected
spiritually by your early experiences of trauma. Find
someone you trust to discuss what you are learning and
feeling. And when you return to reading these pages, we
invite you to allow your full curiosity to develop. As always,
we recommend that you taste everything and swallow only
what you choose.

So take your time. Get comfortable with all you have been
learning and give yourself compassionate understanding,
even as you proceed with these words, even as you proceed
on your journey.

4

Does This Stage Of Recovery Embrace Religion?

God is a metaphor for a mystery that absolutely transcends all human categories of thought (Joseph Campbell, 1986).

Religion as Expression, not Essence

We view spirituality not as religion, although it may include religious observance, but as each of our expressions of what is most sacred about life, of what connects us to the universe. While spirituality may be part of religion, organized religion is not necessarily a part of spirituality.

The root meaning of religion is rebonding, reconnecting and full of devoted care (*American Heritage Dictionary*, 1981). We believe that the expanded awareness characteristic of Genesis is just that: a reaffirmation of bonding, the connection of bonds that externally exist but from which we have become distanced in our awareness.

23

This rebonding results in devoted care to ourselves, others and the universe. It is like resuming relations with what Carl Jung called our "collective unconscious" (1965). An analogy might be neglecting a valued relationship by not attending to it, forgetting it or not being thoughtful. We might ignore the bond, but not break it. Eventually, we return to that friend and find the love still there.

Religion is also defined as the service and worship of God or the supernatural (*American Heritage Dictionary,* 1981). Since Genesis does indeed consist of commitment to a power beyond the self and beyond the visible, observable universe, in this sense it does embrace religion. But to accept Genesis, to accept the existence of a power greater than yourself, and to achieve more subtle and refined levels of consciousness which enrich all aspects of life, requires a commitment to that *Power,* not to a particular religion.

The stage of Genesis speaks to a universal consciousness and recognizes the transcendental unity of all religions. Organized religion, be it practiced inside or outside a house of worship, may or may not be included in Genesis, just as psychotherapy may or may not be included during the recovery. However, moving into this stage of recovery most often leads to some form of outward expression, whether or not it involves organized religion.

Throughout the ages organized religion has served as a major storehouse and resource for spiritual concerns and values, and it has provided a community for spiritual seekers. There are two important benefits offered by organized religion which are difficult to find elsewhere. One is a community that will support your efforts to develop spiritually, where you can surround yourself with like-minded people who value your goals. The second benefit is the availability of a trained or educated teacher called a pastor, rabbi, minister or guru who can offer guidance and be a counselor in spiritual matters.

The Teachings

If you wish to affiliate with an organization (e.g., temple, church), we recommend that you assess its teachings first. Notice if any of its teachings conflict with all you have been learning about your own recovery. Unfortuately, but commonly, many organizations and teachings tell us to "overcome" our feelings and ignore our past. The teaching is that feelings like anger and fear are not acceptable, and should be "sublimated" or in some way not acknowledged or expressed. And some organizations or teachers believe that the past holds no teaching or power, so we should not look back. Be very careful with these teachings. Children of alcoholics and other childhood trauma have already tried that "cure". You have spent enough of your life believing that "negative" feelings are not okay. "Don't look at what happened!" was too often repeated. In recovery you do not need to repeat this self-rejection! If the organization recommends "Don't talk, don't feel, just trust — us", run — don't walk to the nearest exit!

Remember, human emotions are part of your connection to and gift from God. And your past is a lesson. Feelings are okay. Your past is important. Both need to be acknowledged, owned and respected. Remember to remember that your recovery is dependent upon learning to listen to yourself and trust yourself. Even in Genesis, or especially in Genesis, we need to be able to listen to the inner voice and learn what is for us and what is against us, what makes us happy and what makes us sad. How else can we develop that environment in which we can continue to grow, surrounded by people who support our efforts, not undermine them?

THE TEACHERS

We also have a responsibility to remember that our teachers and leaders are human, and we need to question questionable behavior. Many times it seems easier to be ostriches and bury our heads in the sand so we will not have to deal with disillusionment, disappointment or confrontation. But as we have learned in previous stages of recovery, knowledge is the beginning of wisdom. If we deny what we know, we will be unable to use the information.

Watch your teachers to see how they express their values. Behavior speaks louder than words. While someone might have a fabulous explanation as to why he must live in a mansion, begin to wonder whose money he is using. Mine? Yours? God's? Of course if the teacher doesn't hold herself up as a spiritual leader and acknowledges her desire for material wealth, then you have an entirely different situation.

Situations that demand questioning would include times when the teacher's behavior contradicts his or her words. He may claim to be leading a spiritual life, yet engage in activities you consider immoral or unethical. Or perhaps your teacher has previously taken lifelong vows of celibacy and now announces that sex or marriage is allowed in her life. We strongly encourage you to ask about her reasoning and make up your own mind. We believe a great teacher will encourage you to test him, just as a good therapist will welcome inquiries about his expertise and a great leader will hold herself accountable for her behavior. If your teacher asks you for money for "God's work", yet you see that he lives in great luxury or she wears expensive jewelry, wonder about the discrepancy. Money, power and sex are still the three great destroyers — even at the highest levels of spiritual development.

A Rose By Any Other Name

Regardless of whether or not you choose a group to join, and no matter what group it may be, the names are all the one same reality. This universal power has been called by many names throughout history: God, the Source, the Unnameable, Yahweh, All That Is, Atman, Ram, Love, Higher

Power, Soul, The Absolute, Great Spirit, Allah, Tao and Superconsciousness, to name a few. As Gerald Jampolsky (1983) so elegantly states, "Love doesn't care what you call it." It has also been described in a variety of ways with a variety of characteristics. It may be helpful for the reader temporarily to lay aside former concepts of what this power "looks like" or "acts like". As children, many of us developed a notion of God as a powerful and angry man with a flowing white beard sitting in judgment of us someplace in the sky called "Heaven". Genesis is an opportunity to update old experiences, to revise inaccurate ideas.

Another way to imagine this universal power is described in Shirley McLaine's book, *Out On A Limb* (1983):

> . . . there is a force at work that acts as the cohesive element enabling that miniature planetary system (electrons and protons in the atom) to rotate . . . Some of our scientists . . . say there's an energy that fills interatomic space, but they don't know what it is. Even *they* call it the cohesive element of the atom . . . This energy is the Source energy.

So "God" can be viewed as the mysterious, elusive energy that activates the electrons and protons in every atom of every cell of every thing.

It may also be useful to enlarge your concepts, and expand your choices as you proceed in Genesis. There are an infinite variety of ways to conceive of Genesis, because Genesis manifests itself in an infinite variety of ways. And it is your divine gift to unwrap as you choose, as you are guided.

Sometimes a Rose is Not a Rose

As you proceed, develop spiritual relationships with others who can help you see when you are expressing your highest potential. If you travel this journey alone, you may lose sight of the substance, or the difference between religion and spirituality.

The following story may be illustrative: There was once a very religious fellow who was sitting in his house when a major rainstorm began. It rained so hard that the water began to rise all the way up to his front door. As he opened the front door of his house to see how high the water was, a man in a rowboat came by and said, "We're having a flood! Come and get in the rowboat and I will take you to safety." "No," said the fellow, "God will take care of me."

Well, the rains continued until the fellow had to go up to the second floor of his home to remain safe. Another man in a rowboat came by and said, "We're having a flood! Come and get in the rowboat and I will take you to safety." "No," said the fellow, "God will take care of me."

Well, the rains continued until the fellow had to climb up on top of his house to remain safe. A man in a helicopter came by and hollered down, "We're having a flood! Come and get in the helicopter and I will take you to safety." "No," said the fellow, "God will take care of me."

Well, the rains continued and overran the house, the roof and the fellow. Shortly, the man found himself in heaven and there he saw God. Furious, he went up to God and asked why God had forsaken him. He told God that every day he prayed once in the morning, once in the afternoon, and once in the evening. Every week he went to the house of God and worshipped as his religion dictated. And every year he made a pilgrimage to honor God. "Why, then," he asked, "did you abandon me?"

God turned toward him and gently said, "Abandon you? I didn't abandon you. I sent you two rowboats and a helicopter!"

So understand there is a difference between ritual and communion, between talking the talk and walking the walk, between organized religion and spirituality. As E. Stanley Jones says, ". . . let not our cry be, 'Save the Church,' but 'Seek the kingdom' . . . If the Church should perish, the Kingdom would remain" (1972).

The Golden Rule

Thus, Genesis is non-denominational. All people are free to develop their own personal concept of this stage of recovery and of life, and people from all religious backgrounds or no religious background are free to accept or reject it as part of their recovery.

Recently, in response to the question, "Is it necessary to believe in God in order to live the kind of life you are describing (a spiritual life)?" Dr. Gerald Jampolsky replied, "No. It is only necessary to act out of love and kindness towards others" (1985). In other words, following the Golden Rule of "Doing unto others as you would have them do to you" will lead a person into Genesis. ". . . As you would have them do unto you" is also a guidance to love ourselves, and that love is painstakingly developed in the work of the earlier stages, and continues in Genesis.

5

How Does Genesis Relate To The Spiritual Awakening Of Alcoholics Anonymous?

I call the 'still small voice within' the voice of God. You can call it what you will. (Eileen Caddy Findhorn Community, 1980).

The First Awakening

At the beginning of recovery from alcoholism, Steps Two and Three of Alcoholics Anonymous acknowledge a Higher Power and require a "leap of faith" to turn life over to the care of that Power. Early steps in recovery for adult children are also a "leap of faith" that something beyond our day-to-day selves will help. It is an acknowledgment that our lives are unmanageable, that we have been unable to transform them ourselves, and that recovery can be accomplished, but only with help.

One of Bill W.'s earliest followers was a man who was unable to believe in God. Bill decided that if this man could only believe in the power of the small, new fellowship, AA might still be useful to him. That man became sober! (AA World Service, 1973).

Recovery for adult children of alcoholics or trauma accelerates when they enter the stage we have termed Emergent Awareness (Gravitz & Bowden, 1985). Here they become aware of the spiritual, psychological, physiological and genetic vulnerabilities acquired as a result of having an alcoholic parent. Here they acknowledge that their problems in living had their origins in the family system of alcoholism, that they did not and could not control that situation — nor can they now. This recognition prepares the soil for the work to follow and, most importantly, for the recognition of what they *can* change!

What we can control in our adult lives is our view of events and our responses to events. Events do not need to determine our response to them. Indeed, the ways in which we do respond can direct and influence the event more than the event itself (Satir, 1986).

If adult children are unable to hope, unable to believe that something outside themselves may provide strength, then they find it difficult to begin the challenging process of change. To start down a path, one has to sense it will go somewhere. To confidently invest one's money in a business venture, one must have some hope that it will prosper. This initial belief, or hope, is part of what we consider to be the "first awakening".

Many children of alcoholics and other trauma reach adulthood with a death-like belief that life holds only pain or shame. To borrow a phrase, they are living lives of quiet desperation. Their goal becomes to hide their personal reality from others to avoid what they believe will be certain rejection. A client recently stated that she could not tell her therapy group how she really felt because she knew that they would not like her if they knew her better. She is in the difficult early stage of recovery where she still carries a great deal of self-rejection. She feels unacceptable as she is, afraid to believe she can change and afraid of the change itself.

Into this comes the newborn belief that change is possible. This is the hope engendered by the spiritual energy of recovery.

This initial movement toward a positive orientation to life requires a great leap of faith across a chasm of terrible memories and treacherous experiences. As a result of this faith, awareness and energy emerge. The stage of Emergent Awareness is similar to Steps Two and Three in AA, and is an early intimation of a higher awakening or what we consider to be the "second awakening" of Genesis.

So there are at least two major awakenings for adult children of alcoholics and other children of trauma. The first awakening is the *awakening of hope* that help really is possible; it midwifes a *commitment to recovery* and ushers in Emergent Awareness. This enables adult children to take initial steps toward recovery. It is a surrender of despair, a longing for health. It is made from a "bottom" or lowpoint in which the adult child is sick and tired of being sick and tired. Something — Al-Anon, an ACoA group, a book, a conversation — suddenly holds promise. The first awakening is for salvation. It is the "trust" in the "trust and obey" directive for many religions (Wayman, 1986).

Regarding the early spiritual awakening for an alcoholic, Bill W. asked, "Is sobriety all that we are to expect of a spiritual awakening? No, it is only a bare beginning; it is only the first gift of the first awakening. If more gifts are to be received, our awakening has to go on" (Kurtz, 1979).

This initial relationship with a Higher Power or God might be all that gets a person through the beginning stages of recovery. Individuals do not have the option of making a free choice for Genesis as a lifestyle as long as they are still bound by their history and/or their habits. You might start the recovery process and immediately decide, "Now that I know about the impact of alcoholism, I want to help others." The trap, of course, is that early acceptance may result in continuing to avoid the grief and anger that has been denied for so long. And those emotions must be experienced before they can be integrated (Brandon, 1979).

So as you read this, know that any choices you might make at the beginning of your recovery are inherently different from those chosen at a later stage of your healing. Each stage brings a new perspective. And turning your complete energy early in recovery to others or to a spiritual community can be a diversion and an avoidance. Just as AA asks that you work Steps One through 11 before you work 12, so too must you work through Stages One to Five before you focus on the Sixth Stage, Genesis.

The Second Awakening

The second awakening of Genesis is a rededication to life from a position of strength and awareness, not desperation and despair. It is analogous to Steps Eleven and Twelve.

As writer Lillian Smith (Quoted by Rev. Perino, 1981) put it, "There are two journeys every one of us must make: into our own hearts, accepting what we find there; and into the world, accepting it as our home." Genesis is the journey out into the world which we take after we have journeyed inside ourselves, to our own heart and history.

This second awakening of Genesis includes a commitment based on the firm foundation built from the previous stages of recovery and usually follows the experience of Integration. It is the "obey" of the "trust and obey" in that we begin listening and attending to a higher voice and following its path. It repeats Step Three of "turning it over" and is also analogous to Steps Eleven and Twelve of AA. Until the work of the other steps or stages of recovery is done, a rededication of one's life is not really feasible.

We cannot enjoy the blossoming flower until the soil has been prepared, the seeds have been planted, the stem allowed to grow and a bud has appeared. All this takes time, effort and tending. Emergent Awareness (like AA's Step Two) provides the faith to begin the planting. It lets the individual know or suspect that there really is such a thing as a flower, that others have grown them, and he or she really can grow one too. There are cases on record of individuals being swept up into a spiritual state without apparent personal preparation, and a flower seeming to appear out of nowhere, but those instances are rare. Let us not wait. Let us move forward and prepare ourselves by doing the work of the earlier stages. Let us get down on our hands and knees and work in the garden.

The second awakening of Genesis is a dedication beyond the commitment to our own personal recovery, but is dependent upon the fruits of the previous commitment to ourselves. As Bill W.'s physician, Dr. Silkworth, said to Bill, "You've got the cart before the horse, boy . . . first help others to work on the daily, physical issues and maybe then, but only then, will they be ready to listen to this God talk" (Thomsen, 1975). A person in pain finds it difficult to concentrate on the clergyman's sermon.

Bill himself acknowledged a "second conversion experience" that occurred six years after his spiritual awakening in Towns Hospital (Thomsen, 1975). This was the rainy night, during "the winter of Bill's discontent," when the Jesuit priest, Father Ed, appeared. It was the night when two major and lasting events occurred. First, Bill admitted his wrongs and weaknesses to another. He later called it the night he took his Fifth Step. Second, it was also the night Bill was told in no uncertain terms by Father Ed that he was destined to a life of discontent — "divine dissatisfaction" — and that it was God's will that it should be so in order that he would constantly strive to be all he could (AA World Services, Inc., 1984). This affirmation of his life and his drive was very powerful and positive for Bill.

Sometime afterward, Bill had occasion to revisit a number of groups he had received help from. He discovered a similar phenomenon to the second awakening we describe here. He talked to person after person who had initially depended on the Fellowship to avoid dying from alcoholism. They had achieved sobriety and straightened out their lives. Becoming strong and stable, they felt able to depend on themselves. However, after achieving health, some event caused these individuals to view the world through new eyes, rediscovering the principles of AA at a new, higher level (Thomsen, 1975). That event is often a new challenge that initially looks like a "tragedy".

An expression of the second awakening is embodied in Steps 11 and 12 in Alcoholics Anonymous:

> Step 11: Sought through prayer and meditation to improve our conscious contact with God *as we understood Him,* praying only for knowledge of His will for us and the power to carry that out.

> Step 12: Having had a spiritual awakening as the result of these Steps, we tried to carry this message to others, and to practice these principles in all our affairs.

Genesis includes not only Step 11, the *striving* for expanded consciousness, but is also Step 12: *action,* based on the awareness of the underlying unity of all things and the universal essence of that power — love. Indeed, the shades of grey of Genesis are embodied in Steps 1 to 10 as well. The Genesis journey includes that search or experience described in AA's 11th Step as ". . . prayer and meditation to improve our conscious contact . . ." With that second awakening, the individual has traveled through the first five stages of recovery and healing. As a result she or he is able to take a leap forward from that firm foundation into a higher level of living, leaving behind their own will as much as possible and as often as possible.

Step 12 is the application of Genesis: "carry the message" and "practice these principles". It requires continual effort to maintain and expand that second spiritual awakening within our daily lives, just as the recovery process in the early stages requires diligence and frequent recommitment. There becomes an awareness of the spiritual connection which unites us with ourselves, others and the universe.

We also believe that an integral manifestation of living in Genesis is the concept of Step 12's "carry the message". By this we do not mean that you must tell everyone you meet about your spiritual journey. On the contrary, we strongly recommend that you continue to use the share-check-share strategy learned in previous stages of recovery (Gravitz & Bowden, 1985), and share with those who have ears to hear. Rather, to "carry the message" more appropriately requires a commitment to a heartfelt project, be it ministering to the poor or the homeless, donating time to a special cause, serving on the board of directors for an organization meaningful to you, working for world peace, being a healthy role model for your child or even watching a sunset. Genesis demands expression, and will lead you to your place of service. The paradox is that this service is both a manifestation of, and an impetus to, the experience of Genesis. One client told us that she did not realize the purpose of her painful childhood in an alcoholic family until she observed the fruits of her work with other children of trauma.

Time Is Required

Rather than a dramatic flash of lights accompanying a rapid and total change in personality, we have observed what psychologist William James has called the "educational variety" of awakening (1902). It develops slowly over a period of time. It frequently includes two discrete passages that are analogous to the first and second awakening. The first, *surrender* out of desperation, a struggling away from pain: trust that change can happen. The second, *dedication* out of a deeply committed love and a striving toward universal integrity: *obeying the higher guidance.*

The following poem describes this surrender as well as dedication in another way by using the concepts of the "Dream" and the "Journey":

Both are important,
The Journey and the Dream,
The coming-out and the entering-in.

Without the Journey
The Dream is a futile entering into yourself
Where you ride a monotonous wheel
That spins around you alone.
With the Journey
The entering-in is itself a Journey
That does not end inside you
But passes through the self and
Out the other side of you
When you ride the wheel
You found inside.
To remain inside too long
Makes the Journey a fairytale Odyssey
And the Dream becomes illusion.
The wheel must spin on the real road
Where your Dream leads you.

To remain on the road too long
Dims the Dream
Until you no longer see it
And the road replaces the Dream.

The Journey and the Dream
Are one balanced act of love
And both are realized
Outside the mind.

(Bodo, 1972)

The Dream is the step of faith first taken in early recovery, the first awakening. The Journey is the commitment to action, to obeying that higher choice, to living out that faith and belief system of the second awakening, or the 11th and 12th Steps.

A metaphor may make the first and second awakenings even clearer. Imagine people who have been raised in a northern climate and have never seen or felt fire. They have been cold all their lives except for rare and brief occasions when the sun comes out long enough to remove the surface chill. For generations they have believed that life is just cold, that everyone everywhere lives like they do: cold and uncomfortable. Then one day a small flame is introduced to the forested compound in which they live. At first they have a variety of reactions, including surprise, disbelief, fear, anger and then relief. Surprise results from the newness of it; fear in not knowing what it is or what to expect; disbelief comes because the warmth goes against all they have ever known; anger comes from having all their old beliefs thrown into question and in discovering there have existed alternatives to cold. But because it feels right and good, relief is also experienced.

This is the first awakening — a roller coaster of feelings, and the dawning belief that warmth really is possible! Although many mornings they awaken with the question, "Is there really a fire or did I just dream it? Has it gone away? Dare I believe?", they learn to believe.

Over time, they learn to keep the fire burning and to keep warm by the fire, fanning that flame day after day until it is roaring and healthy. It warms them whenever they come near. They learn the characteristics or issues of fire; they transform their behaviors, building in daily tasks to tend the flame; and slowly warmth and fire become integrated in their lifestyle.

As the fire grows and time passes, they discover they can create fire by means of rubbing sticks together, and that they can carry the fire to other places. The chill, the cold, become a way of the past and they are free of their old view of the world.

Similar to this is the Tibetan master's rite of passage to stand on a freezing mountain top at 17,000 feet above sea level. Cold, wet blankets are draped around him. Using only the resources within his body, he is to dry the wet blankets not once, but three times. The rite of passage is to discover the great power within the self and the universe. Like the Tibetan master, our above imagined people learn a way to create their own heat. And this is their second awakening. They become free to leave the compound and to be warm wherever they stop to build a fire. Had they refused to trust those strange, moving flames and left the compound before learning about fire and heat, they would have remained forever cold, never having the opportunity to discover the essential process.

6

What Is Life Like In Genesis?

*God is always visible the moment the inward eye is
clear (Rufus N. Jones).*

Fullness and Joy Result

In Genesis, we are conscious of what we believe in and
make an effort to express our highest values. Our life will
reflect what we believe, and by the time we arrive here, we
believe in recovery and the significance of life. As a lifestyle,
Genesis would find a person taking time daily to honor their
humanness, to appreciate the universe and to give and share
with others. "Small" actions and "small" interactions are
given consideration in terms of how they will affect the
world (which, of course, includes ourselves). Genesis
involves a conscious commitment to live a life of love.

The experience of Genesis is unique to each person. It
varies from person to person and from time to time within
each person. Nevertheless, there seem to be common
elements. Life seems fuller, more purposeful. There seem to
be an external/internal companion and guide. The relationship with self, others and the universe includes a new,

deeper dimension. Extraordinary awareness and consciousness emerge along with an increasing sense of well-being.
The awareness of connection with everything and everyone
begins to be primary. Many may experience this awareness
as a generalized feeling of joy, love and peace. There is a
famous saying in *The Upanishads* which embodies this: "I
am that, thou are that, all this is nothing but that!" This
saying is a reminder to us that everything is from God — and
everyone is part of God.

A Shift in Awareness

Our awareness has two fundamental aspects. One is the
outer mind or the everyday objective mind of rational
consciousness which by its very nature must be selective
and limited. This awareness is bounded, relative and ever-
changing in its nature. The second is the inner mind which
views life and the universe as unbounded, absolute and
never changing in its nature. This may become an inherent
part of the way we view the world, but our experience of
that awareness will most likely be intermittent. It is similar
to having the knowledge that we are on a particular planet
which circles a particular sun which is but one sun in a
particular solar system of which there are countless others.
We may have this information but not always experience the
awesomeness of this truth. The *experience* of this awareness
may only last for brief periods of time, stimulated by out of
the ordinary events or seeming miracles.

One woman told us of entering a room in her summer
home where she was caring for a sick plant. As she removed
the invading mites from the leaves of the plant she
discovered unusually large drops of water on the leaves here
and there. Knowing no one had been in the house but her,
so no one had watered the plant, she was suddenly moved
to an emotional experience of God's presence — of the
absolute, unlimited possibilities — and was filled with
gratitude. God had left a "calling card". Consciousness

which includes the experience of the *relative* together with the *absolute* is sometimes referred to as "cosmic consciousness", universal consciousness or God consciousness.

Eastern religions teach methods for attaining and maintaining this awareness. Mahatma Gandhi (1957) practiced God consciousness daily, and East Indians believe that he immediately attained union with God at his death because as he fell to the ground dying, his final gesture to his murderer was to bring his hands together in the prayer position. This particular gesture in India is used in combination with the word "Namaste" which means "I bow to the God within you." Even in the throes of death Gandhi's mind turned to God.

Universal awareness is historically the primary way to a peaceful existence. When we remind ourselves of our connection to all other living beings, we experience compassion for others. Hatred and destruction become absurd, while peace for all becomes eminently sensible. Religious scriptures advise: "Thou dost keep him in perfect peace whose mind is stayed on thee" (Isaiah 26:3). This philosophy of life can be translated literally, as Gandhi taught, to keep our mind on God at all times. The result would be peacefulness. As we increase our own sense of peace, we begin to treat others more peacefully and so it goes.

We start practicing in the same way as we practice all new behaviors in the earlier stages of recovery. Step by step we begin training ourselves, for example, to think of God or feel peace one second in the morning and one second in the evening before bed. Then we begin to increase these times, perhaps by adding a reading of something inspirational in the middle of the day, or learning a song about God that we hum. And on and on.

This is similar to the process of one of our clients who learned to experience his feelings. Initially he reported that he was unaware of what he felt or experienced and wanted to have feelings. We advised him to first make a list of any feelings of which he was aware. Next, he selected one time of day to listen to himself and assess his feelings. And then we helped him expand his list. In the evening he would go over the events of the day, asking himself what he felt in various situations. If that did not help, he was to ask himself what his best friend would have felt in those same situations. Next, he monitored his feelings three times a day, increasing the amount of time he noticed his feelings. Finally, he checked within himself at numerous intervals throughout the day. More and more often, he found himself becoming aware of feelings in the present. This allowed him to let others know of his reactions if he chose to tell them. He had increased his resources. So too, can we train ourselves to be conscious of our connection to God.

God consciousness may also be translated as a training of our minds to focus and refocus on loving, being and giving service. We teach ourselves to keep thoughts of love or ways to help others in our mind more and more. Or we practice being here and now, that is, living in the moment instead of in the past or the future. We practice being a human *being*, rather than a human *doing*.

A paradox in following the spiritual path is the difference between being and doing. For some, simply being is the ultimate spiritual lifestyle. People living Genesis from this perspective may be found in daily meditation in a Himalayan cave or a religious monastery. For others, spirituality is a lifestyle of doing, of expressing, of manifesting God's will in the world. It includes daily action and interaction within society, such as working for a social service agency, child care center or treating each person met with respect and love. Both paths reflect Genesis.

When grounded in expanded consciousness, a person is free to appreciate his or her surroundings more completely. Experiences are approached as potential teachers, and what initially may be seen as pain can be perceived as a gift. We can learn to control how we respond to events, and continually seek out the lessons to be learned from each experience.

Although life continues to bring the good and the bad, the person in Genesis maintains an evenness of temperament.

She or he experiences fewer and fewer peaks and valleys. Life's events are seen as secondary to the miracle of existence and God. Several times in the Christian scriptures, Jesus exhorts his followers, ". . . do not be anxious." This directive or exhortation is a demand of faith. We are asked to have faith that we will be cared for, fed and sheltered.

> Consider the lilies of the field, how they grow; they neither toil nor spin; yet I tell you even Solomon in all his glory was not arrayed like one of these. But if God so clothes the grass of the field, which today is alive and tomorrow is thrown into the oven, will he not much more clothe you.
>
> (Mat 6: 28-30).

This is a new level of trust and faith. It requires us to step forward even when we cannot see where our foot will land. It calls us to run with our eyes closed. So life in Genesis will be more peaceful, less worrisome and certainly less controlled by us.

A Shift in Perspective

A woman we know experienced the cataclysmic event of an accident resulting in the paralysis of her daughter. As she dealt with the grief, the physicians, the hospitals, others affected around her, and in particular with her critically injured daughter, she paradoxically began to experience frequent periods of heightened intimacy, peace and joy. This response began to flourish between daughter and mother, family and friends. People who initially arrived upset, anxious and afraid to enter the hospital room left with wide-eyed wonder. They felt relieved and reassured by the love and strength they witnessed. Shortly after the accident, mother and daughter lay together in the hospital bed. The young woman quietly said to her mother, "I have learned so much from this that I'm actually glad it happened. Do you know what I mean?"

Within days, the "medical diagnosis" was that a massive system of denial was being established. When physicians walked into the intensive care room and witnessed the young woman and guests holding hands, smiling, laughing, sharing love and serenity, they made chart notes on the "emotional difficulties" being experienced. But as the profound sense of love spread, touching even the Intensive Care Unit nurses, it became ever clearer that the "tragedy" had offered this family a new opportunity, another vision of life's meaning.

Invariably, people who experience Genesis notice a fundamental and characteristic change in the overall quality of their living. They begin to appreciate each event in their lives as right and meaningful. Feelings of well-being, peace, and joy visit the heart more and more often. Some have likened this emotional experience to being "high" on drugs. It is a natural high.

Not My Will

In the stage of Genesis, we become aware that we do not travel on this journey alone, nor need we be totally buffeted by what happens to us. Rather we become *conscious co-creators* with a Higher Power. This path is tenderly described in the following words written at the ending of a pilgrimage in India and the beginning of the next spiritual journey in America.

> I will be very sad to leave here — but it is not my will any longer that matters; it is only the divine will that is of importance or lasting value. These things are not for my sake, but for the sake of the Divine. I do not lay down the conditions of service — I seek only the privilege of serving . . . joyfully. Wherever He wants me.
>
> (Loved One, 1986)

For mature spirituality, we must learn to distinguish between the wish fulfillments of our own ego or impulsiveness (dead-end or negative paths) and the guidance of the Higher Power. It is sometimes very difficult to know what the universe desires of us. We may feel pulled in a certain direction; yet, we wonder if it is our Higher Power or our own ego (that personal sense of who we are which is bounded by our senses).

Children of alcoholics especially may stumble on the old feelings of not trusting themselves. Trained in the childhood home to deny their internal experience, all children of trauma must relearn the vital connection between their inner and outer experiences. This necessitates work and time in the earlier stages of recovery and the development of simple techniques such as meditation and introspection to connect with the Higher Self or God.

As a general rule, if a teaching leads you to harmful thoughts or actions against yourself or others, it is not from a universal or Higher Power. Here a tested, trusted friend or consultant is useful. To develop useful sources of guidance, find someone trustworthy who can offer feedback on what is happening to you. Utilize the share-check-share strategy (Gravitz & Bowden, 1985). Start by sharing just a little bit of yourself or just a little information about this aspect of your journey. Then pay attention. Become hypervigilent. Keep your eyes up, keep your ears open and, above all, validate what happens inside of you. If you begin to feel small or dumb, consider what the other person just did or said to you. Based on that, decide if you want to share more. If you begin to feel good inside, honored, then perhaps you will choose to share a little bit more. By taking it a step at a time and avoiding all-or-none phenomena, you can select the people who will be supportive of your spiritual development and identify those who will not. You can develop relationships with friends who will be helpful consultants on the issues that come up as you travel along the road of recovery.

Changing Relationships

Relationships in this context are increasingly the creation of love, becoming opportunities to confront areas in the self which are limited. A person living Genesis is freer from negative experiences of the past and more able to enjoy enriching involvement with everything and everyone around him. There is an enhanced inner stability and sanctuary from events which are subject to change.

You may also find that some of your friends are not interested in taking the journey into spirituality. While you may choose to continue your relationship with them, learn where you will and will not be understood through share-check-share. Be exceedingly wary of the feeling or belief that it is your assignment to "bring them around" and introduce them to God. There can be a great deal of arrogance in that belief. Trust that if they need to learn certain lessons, they will ask for what they need. And if you cannot trust someone to ask for what they need, take the time to evalute your relationship with that person and reconsider the friendship. Here again some friends may be left behind and you may experience that same fear, loneliness, guilt and isolation that you experienced in earlier stages of recovery as you let go of old, ill-fitting relationships. It is a bridge that must be crossed.

And through your insecurity know that special new friends are even now moving toward you to share this part of the journey. Space must be made for them. People who are seeking the spiritual life must be invited into your heart. Our environment absolutely does affect us, and a big part of our environment is our friends, those people with whom we spend time. You must ensure that much of your environ-ment supports and encourages the development of your higher self. The entire recovery process is necessary because of the simple facts that our environment affects us and our first environment was filled with disease and addiction. So once again, we must readjust and "fine tune" our environment so that rather than deal with addiction in our personal relationships, we deal with health and healing.

One of the things you may notice about your life in Genesis is that increasingly you will be surrounded by very special, spiritual people. Just as the recovering alcoholic begins to meet and know others whose lifestyle is not dependent on drugs, so too can you cultivate relationships with people who share your values and views. Utilize the strategy of share-check-share to determine who your intimates in this area will be. Watch. Listen. Observe. Discover how you feel with this or that person. Listen to how he or she responds to you and then listen to your nervous system.

You may also find you have friends who believe you should only experience or express positive feelings. One of our clients describes this as wanting to be in "La-La Land" all the time. You have several choices in these relationships. You may continue these relationships with the limitation of only expressing part of yourself, perhaps withholding certain emotions that you experience (for even in Genesis, people continue to be people and experience the full range of human emotions).

Another choice is that you may terminate these relationships. Or you may continue them, and continue to be yourself, expressing all that you are, all that you feel, but without the other person sharing back or appreciating your willingness to work or change the relationship. None is the "perfect" solution. And, of course, you may choose one thing now, then choose another later. It really is up to you.

One of our clients, after seven years in recovery, had a conflict with her very best friend from childhood. They had both been working on their spiritual development and recovery. Our client had learned to express her feelings clearly as soon as she was able. When she did so, however, she discovered that her dear friend had taught herself that feelings like anger were bad and should not be discussed. Rather, they should be "overcome". She did not want to talk about it, because she considered it "increasing the darkness." Our client did not know what to do. She was pleased that she could express herself to someone as important as her best friend. She felt she had risked a lot and that it was scarey to say how she felt. She had hoped they could then talk about it and perhaps make some changes in the relationship that would make it stronger and more comfortable. She hoped it was a passing difficulty, which both could learn from by communicating. She decided to continue the friendship and watch what happened.

Unfortunately a year later a similar issue recurred and our client again spoke up, expressing her anger. Again her friend called it "darkness" and refused to talk about it. Our client had the choice to accept the relationship with its limitation of their being unable to discuss problems that included "negative" feelings or she could say "good-bye" to a friend of many years. Our client chose to continue the relationship, but with caution over what she shared and with a personal agreement to herself that whenever the issue appeared, she would address it directly and let it go, expecting no change or understanding from her friend. What ensued was a relationship with much less intimacy. Our client experienced grief over the loss, but continued to be unwilling to quietly subject herself to her friend's behavior.

You may find that even some of your newer friends slip away the further you travel. Decisions have to be made as to whether you want to maintain each relationship or not. To not make a decision is to make a decision. There is no right and wrong here. Whatever you believe is best in the circumstances is your most trusted guide.

Consider Before Speaking

It is important to learn the meaning of the biblical quote along the way in earlier stages and again in Genesis: "Do not give dogs what is holy; and do not throw your pearls before swine lest they trample them under foot and turn to attack you" (Mat. 7:6). All-or-none functioning would have you believe that to be honest you must share all that is happening to you spiritually. Do not be deceived. There are two major reasons to discriminate with whom, where and when you share your experiences.

Just as it is unwise to sell arms and ammunition to a country that will use them to attack you, it is unwise to share tender, vulnerable experiences and feelings with someone who will use them against you later to tease you, diminish you or criticize you. That is the point of the St. Matthew quote above.

For instance, early in recovery it is unwise to phone your unrecovering alcoholic father and say: "Dad, I have the most wonderful news! I have just read a book on adult children of alcoholics and discovered that I am not alone and it is not my fault! And your alcoholism is a disease!" You may of course do that, but you need to be prepared to hear, "What the hell are you talking about? What do you mean, my alcoholism? Are you going off on one of your self-righteous trips again? I tell you, you are just going to have to learn to handle your life yourself. You have to grow up, you have to . . ." and on it goes. If you are ready to handle that, fine. Call. Also ask yourself why you are calling, however.

Similarly, to tell someone that you feel you have accomplished a great deal of recovery and are now embarking on a new life dedicated to the spiritual can be wonderful — if they have a healthy love for you, and if they have ears to hear. This is another place where you continue to share-check-share. See how you are treated. Notice if, for instance, a week later they make a comment about how "arrogant you have become now that you are recovered and better than others."

Honor the Holy

The second reason to be thoughtful about sharing certain experiences of Genesis is that they are sacred. They are not for public consumption. They are the result of the increasing bond between God and you, and they function to increase that bond further. They are a result of, and a cause of, that closeness. To talk about them may dilute them. To talk about them may be to give them away. This can be exceedingly difficult for adult children of alcoholics and other childhood trauma who are used to sharing everything. Nothing was ever just ours except terrible, shameful secrets. In Genesis, a new lesson is to share some beautiful things only with great care. Openness and honesty are not the same.

The authors have noticed as our own lives have become more attuned to Genesis that our clients now experience freedom to talk about their spiritual lives. It seems similar to what counselors discovered about the topic of sex. Before the counselor became comfortable with that area of life, clients never brought it up as a concern. After counselors received training or changed their attitude to one of openness, clients suddenly began identifying sex as an important issue, even when the therapist had not mentioned it! So you may notice others spontaneously sharing with you their spiritual experiences. Each time you carefully share this part of yourself, it will be strengthened.

7

If I Experience Genesis, Will I Finally Get To Be Perfect?

I feel unbalanced, always going to extremes without any middle ground. It's always either-or with me. I feel unhappy inside a lot of the time, even though outwardly I have a lot going for me. I always feel inside like I'm not good enough, not smart enough and not pretty enough. I guess I feel like I should be perfect. (Anonymous Adult Child of an Alcoholic, 1985).

It's Not All or Nothing

Alas! There is no perfection, even in Genesis. Perfection, when defined as constant expanded consciousness, belongs to a rare few, known down through the ages as supremely enlightened beings. While Genesis is certainly characterized by joy, deep calm, serenity and even bliss, it is not constant.

Genesis is the *awareness* of the perfect state or the character
of God and a striving for closeness or alignment with that
way of being. For brief periods of time you may find yourself
experiencing a "perfect state of being", but for most of us it
will be fleeting and will serve as a motivator to continue
developing spiritual awareness. A useful affirmation is "I will
live today as best I can. Tomorrow I will do even better"
(Wayman, 1986).

Even most mystics and yogis are unable to stay in
expanded states of awareness and consciousness constantly.
Rephrasing an old proverb, "Before we seek Allah, we must
tether our camels." Clothes need to be cleaned, checkbooks
balanced, groceries bought. Family and friends die. As long
as we inhabit physical bodies, we will have digestive
problems, a car that breaks down, or a stubbed toe. And
often these events pull our consciousness from the sublime
to the mundane. Even a stubbed toe, however, may be seen
as something to be appreciated — a lesson perhaps to slow
down and see what is in the world around us. And when we
utilize the higher conscious and perceive our lives through
that expanded vision, it leads us to a different perspective.
All too often we approach balancing the checkbook with the
same level of emotion as more truly serious matters.

Genesis is not an all-or-none phenomenon nor an all-or-
none state. You are not either living it completely or not
living it at all. It does not start at some precise moment, such
as the end of the Integration stage. Nor do we ever complete
or finish it. From the very beginning what we call Genesis is
residing in us and working for our recovery. However, we
often fail to recognize its presence. It typically happens a
little here and a little there and a little now.

The question of perfection is a critical one for almost
every child of an alcoholic or other trauma. The core issue
of all or none can be subtle, seductive and very patient. It
waits until we are tired or stressed or busy. Just when we
think we have finally mastered it, finally stopped using
black-and-white terms, it trips us again. This might manifest
in a desire to radically alter your life in an extreme fashion,

such as a hasty or poorly thought out decision to sell your home and donate everything to charity.

There may in fact come a point in your spiritual development when you will need to make an all-or-none decision like, "Shall I move to Calcutta and work full-time with Mother Theresa?" or "Shall I become celibate?" or "Shall I join a monastic order to dedicate my life to God?" While one of these might be just the right thing for you to do, it requires much preparation and thought. These decisions are usually not appropriate during the first few years in Genesis. If it becomes time for such a decision, many signs will appear to let you know.

All-or-none also may plague you with self-judging thoughts. For example, believing that if you are not in prayer or meditation 24 hours a day, or eating organic foods, or saying 10 Hail Mary's before each meal, then you are failing to "give your all". Harsh self-judgment is *not* a sign of the spiritual life. Nor are rituals the actual lesson or goal. They are merely guides to the lesson.

All-or-none can create great discouragement if you insist on judging your progress with that yardstick. One client working in the stage of Genesis came in complaining that she was making no progress. We asked her how she had concluded that. She answered, "Last night I woke up in the middle of the night because a moth flew into my hair. As I became awake, I brushed it away quickly and felt frightened. It wasn't until I was fully awake that I considered that moth was part of God and that there is nothing to be afraid of since all is God. The fact that I awakened afraid tells me I'm still unrecovered!"

We reminded her of the subtle and insidious nature of all-or-none, and we also reminded her of several issues she had successfully worked on earlier in her recovery using the technique of "chunking it down".

Chunking it down (Gravitz & Bowden, 1985) is the strategy of taking a specific goal or task, such as wanting to keep your mind in God consciousness, and dividing it into component parts or seeing it in smaller pieces or chunks.

After reminding her of what she already knew, we gave her the homework assignment of using her hypervigilance to watch for any other areas or instances where her all-or-none thinking was sneaking up on her.

Finding balance is an especially difficult issue for all-or-none thoughts, actions and feelings. Even after years of recovery, the old all-or-none functioning can make sorrow for the best of us. Many people will need help from a consultant (e.g., minister, rabbi, guru, spiritual therapist) to keep this path of devotion in balance and filled with joy. If you find yourself saying unkind or derogatory things to yourself, get suspicious. If you find yourself feeling greatly inadequate or incompetent again, get suspicious. If you refuse to take care of daily tasks in order to do spiritual practices all day, get suspicious. Look for the all-or-none functioning and then reevaluate your perspective. You may decide to become more gentle with yourself.

All-or-none also may fuel the desire to skip stages, leading you from Emergent Awareness right into dedicating your life to God and prayer, or commitment to a teacher or religious community without going through the time-consuming and difficult work of reclaiming your own history and developing a sense of discrimination. This leads to tragedies such as the Jim Jones following who gave up their decision-making powers to another human being. And in the late 1970s gave up their lives because he so directed.

External Support

A related concern is how to live Genesis in the midst of a secular, materialistic culture. Some have concluded that spirituality, love and commitment cannot flourish in Western society with its powerful emphasis on competition, wealth and material consumption. We believe, however, that this is another example of all-or-none thinking. It is possible to develop the spiritual aspects of yourself through personal conviction and a lifestyle that includes daily meditation, dialogue with others who share spiritual concerns and a regular refocusing on what you consider to be important. Accept at the outset that it will not be easy, but it will be possible.

The challenge of Genesis is similar to the challenge of the alcoholic's sobriety. He or she knows that society not only condones, but encourages drinking. Abstinence is actually threatening to many other drinkers, because it calls their own drinking into question. There is often a deliberate attempt to get the recovering alcoholic to drink again. We have all heard, "Aw, come on. One drink never hurt anybody." Every day there will be distractions or seductions to pull you from your commitment. Every day you may need to recommit.

The Real American Dream

Curiously, despite concerns over the materialism and lack of spirituality in America, some other cultures consider that the inception of America was truly spiritual and that we, as a people, are destined to emerge as leaders in the spiritual development of the world. East Indians, for example, seem to have a greater respect for American tradition than many Americans. They remind us that the founders of America embarked on the Mayflower seeking freedom to worship God in their own way. And today the words *e pluribus unum* (one out of many) are etched on all our coins, and "In God We Trust" is printed on our treasury notes. These we send into every avenue of world trade (Spalding, 1924).

So let us act as if that were true. Growing and living in Genesis can be the manifestation of that hope, the dream of the founders of this country and a validation for this great experiment called democracy.

Internal Support

So, yes, you can live Genesis within our society. It just will not be easy and it will not be perfect. Take it one step at a time. Remember to remember the slogan, "One day at a time." In fact, there will be times when you will need to take it one minute at a time. For instance, you may find yourself wanting to be particularly sensitive or understanding in the midst of an important conversation with someone.

A woman we were working with described the following visit to her mother. The woman had expressed her concern about her mother's drinking.

> She told me she didn't think it was any of my business since I wasn't living at home anymore. And as far as she was concerned, she wasn't hurting anyone. As I sat next to her, listening to her words, I whispered silently to God through my sadness: 'Please help me really hear and stay centered in my life's purpose of living Genesis and giving love.' I repeated this many times during the conversation. It helped me stay clear and let go of needing her to change.

To Err Is Human

People have a strong tendency to confuse "perfection" with "divineness". They are never the same. Even as you discover that the route to divineness is through your humanness, the route to humanness is through your divineness. All-or-none inevitably leads to despair, impatience and loss of faith. Even in Genesis, we need to be gentle to ourselves and continue to allow ourselves to be human. There is an old saying: "To err is human; to forgive is divine." In crossword puzzles the verb "to err" is often given as a clue for the word "human". Remember the answer to that puzzle. Allow yourself to be human. After all, it is your birthright. You were born into a human body. To help you remember, realize that if God wanted you to be an angel, you would have wings.

It is also helpful to remember that even the chosen disciples of Jesus were unable to maintain their balance and belief. As he spoke to the crowds on a hill near Tiberius, some travelers came and began harassing Jesus and challenging him, saying, "Prove yourself! Show us miracles!" His disciples did likewise. And even after three years of his ministry, as he and his disciples walked toward Jerusalem for the last time, the disciples argued among themselves who would sit at his right hand and who would sit at his left. And on their last night with him, James, John and Peter fell asleep after he had implored them to remain awake with him on that fateful night. And Peter, known as his leader and who was the founder of the Roman Catholic Church, renounced him three times after he was arrested and after swearing to Jesus he would do no such thing, that it was unthinkable!

If the disciples, who were in the personal company of their great teacher could not lead perfect lives, know for certain that we cannot. We are reminded of the comment of former President Jimmy Carter who stated that he had "lusted in his heart". He was acknowledging that even in the highest office of the land there is what he considered human weakness. And we have certainly had that proven often in this century. If the truth be told, all of us, including the great teachers, gurus, ministers and rabbis, have had horrible thoughts. And were we liable for every criminal or bad thought, we would all be in jail or be dead.

So know you are in good company in your imperfection. And accept forgiveness for yourself. For if the truth were known, you have already been forgiven long ago. All we are called to do is to get up every time we fall down, to just keep trying. That means that if you fall short of the mark today, renew your efforts tomorrow. St. Paul wrote the Philippians, "I am not perfect, I am simply pressing on to the upward call of God." (Phil. 3:12)

Charles Whitfield (1985) makes an important distinction between the Higher Self (unity, compassion, understanding and acceptance) and the lower self (power, passion and survival). He states that to be constantly in the Higher Self is to neglect the frequent, chronic distress affecting the lower self, such as the need for food, warmth and so on. The sages say, "Seek Allah, but tether your camel first." To be our

Higher Self authentically, Whitfield states, is to be totally aware of our lower self and to take care of it.

An old saying tells us that the cosmically aware person lives 200% of life: 100% inner, spiritual glory and 100% outer, material concerns. And we can know that it is inevitably an approximation.

Choose Positive Responses

There is an old tale of a prince who cut his foot while hunting with a companion. His friend, a sage, looked at the cut as the prince sat moaning and said, "All is for the good." The prince, enraged at his friend's callousness, pushed him into a nearby well. From the bottom of the well, the friend hollered, "All is for the good." The exasperated prince rode toward home, but was shortly caught by enemies who planned to offer the prince to their gods as a sacrifice. At just that moment before the prince was to be killed, the priest spied the hunting wound and immediately ordered the prince released saying, "This man is unfit for our Gods; he is not perfect!"

The prince remorsefully returned to his friend who was still in the well. As he pulled him out of the well, he told his friend everything that had happened. The prince concluded by saying, "You were right; my accident was for the good." But then, seeing his friend damp and dirty, said, "But what about you? I pushed you into this horrible well! Everything isn't for the good after all!"

"Ah," said the friend, "You are wrong. Everything is for the good. If you had not pushed me in the well, surely I would have ridden back with you. Then I too would have been captured and, having no cut, I would have been sacrificed! Yes, all is for the good."

To state the obvious, which adult children of alcoholics and other children of trauma need to hear again and again, we cannot control all that befalls us, even under the best of conditions. But we *can* choose how we will react to events and how we will deal with each experience. One of the practical benefits of Genesis is reflected in the following quote:

> . . . it is an aspect of problem solving wherein you see that there are no problems, only experiences. And by seeing the reality of your experience, you benefit from it, and you become very thankful for that experience and you anticipate your next experience with joy and thanksgiving. (John-Roger, 1985)

Even when we embrace this philosophy, however, we will still find ourselves occasionally cursing some event or situation that comes along.

Dr. Gerald Jampolsky, who often lectures on how to keep only love in your heart, tells his story of arriving at an airport with ticket in hand, only to be informed that his flight was overbooked and he would not be able to fly. His immediate reaction was anger, and he began to argue with the attendant. The friend with him, Diane, leaned over and softly spoke a line from one of his books: "Would you rather be right or would you rather be happy?" Jerry's reaction turned to rage, but as he turned to his friend, he caught her eye and saw the humor in the situation and the uselessness of his anger. He allowed himself to take a deep breath and began to calm down. He let go of his anger. As a result, not only did he feel better, but he was selected to take one of the few remaining seats. As the attendant put it, "You were the only person who didn't harass me while you were waiting."

Who's Better?

It is important to understand that people who experience Genesis or Genesis phenomena are not better than those who do not. They simply experience a different consciousness, a different awareness, a different reality. Resist judging and you will proceed more quickly. It is good to remember the paradox that when the time is right, the path will be revealed to you. In the meantime, of course, it helps to keep your eyes open.

8

Are There Other Pitfalls In Genesis?

A man stood on a mountain top. He spread his arms. "God," he cried, "fill me with your light!" A voice answered, "I have been filling you with my light. But you keep leaking!" (Millman, 1987).

Discipline and Sloth

Perhaps no one has more clearly described the two major pitfalls of sloth and lack of discipline as M. Scott Peck in the classic *The Road Less Traveled.* Laziness, which Peck defines as the opposite of love, is considered the ultimate impediment to spiritual growth.

"If we overcome laziness," says Peck, "all other impediments will be overcome. If we do not overcome laziness, none of the others will be hurdled" (Peck, 1978). Spiritual growth is an effortful process. To remain on the spiritual path, God must always be a co-creator. As Peck stated (1978):

In debating the wisdom of a proposed course of action, human beings routinely fail to obtain God's side of the issue.

63

They fail to consult or listen to the God within them, the knowledge of rightness which inherently resides within the minds of all mankind. We make this failure because we are lazy. It is work to hold these internal debates. They require time and energy . . .

Peck goes on to point out a major form that laziness takes is fear. Much of our fear consists of the fear of changing the status quo. We become afraid to take in information which does not fit our well-established model of the world. Once we take in the reality of Genesis, among other things, our entire sense of and meaning of responsibility radically changes. Again quoting Peck, he notes:

For to experience one's closeness to God is also to experience the obligation to God, to be the agent of His power and love. The call to grow is a call to a life of effortful caring, to a life of service and whatever sacrifice seems required (1978).

Discipline, on the other hand, is the basic set of tools we need to solve life's problems constructively. Without discipline, we insist on getting everything *now*. We have trouble accepting personal responsibility for our actions, we avoid the truth as well as fail to see reality accurately and we have no way to prioritize life's demands on us. Discipline is a system of techniques including meditation, yoga, biofeedback, autogenic training and psychotherapy. With discipline we can delay gratification, be responsible, be truthful and be balanced (Peck, 1978).

We have found both of these pitfalls make their appearance over and over. For example, we have experienced a tendency to talk ourselves out of actions, like meditation, that we know are good for us.

"After all," we tell ourselves, "we're tired. We've been working hard all day; we can do it tomorrow."

The mind constantly talks to us. So we won't pray; we won't remember to remember there really is something larger than us. We put off our meditation until we really *are* too tired to concentrate well, or we eat something heavy just before meditating which interferes with the process. The same can be true with our daily exercise program. It is easier to let things go in the same manner as we let the breakfast dishes go, or left the bed unmade, or let the laundry pile up. It seems that all things seek to go to rest, but growth requires a constant recommitment. In the same fashion as you have kept yourself motivated to *get* to Genesis, those same techniques will be useful again to stay *in* Genesis. Live one day at a time, sometimes one moment at a time.

If one of your goals is to incorporate meditation into your daily routine, start slowly. One way to bypass the mind's complaining is to agree to meditate for only a moment. You don't have to meditate a long time, just a minute or two. But often you will find yourself wanting to continue the meditation once you have begun. It is usually getting started that is most difficult.

Loss of Faith

Loss of faith, which is often expressed as impatience, is another way of looking at laziness. Remember, success can be defined as getting up one more time than you fall down. There are many "falls from grace" in this stage, and those who seek higher awareness must affirm and re-affirm their volition. Determination is neither all or none nor is it achieved just once.

"Dry periods" can be particularly difficult. When you have been praying, meditating, studying and giving of yourself for months and then come to a period of time when you feel lonely and out of touch with your Higher Power, it requires great faith and patience to continue the practices until you come out on the other side, again feeling the bond with the universal. And if anything is worth your time and deserves your patience it is spiritual growth.

As author Og Mandino (1968) states:

> Time teaches all things to he who lives forever, but I have not the luxury of eternity. Yet within my allotted time I must practice the art of patience, for nature acts never in haste. To create the olive, king of all trees, a hundred years is required. An onion plant is old in nine weeks. I have lived as an onion plant. It has not pleased me. Now I wouldst become the greatest of olive trees.

Dry periods can be viewed as rest points, necessary for integrating all that has been occurring. It is like climbing a series of mountains. It is wise to pause as you reach a flat, sheltered spot and catch your breath. It is a good time to look back, see where you came from and notice how far you have traveled. Then when you are rested and readied, you continue on.

Darkness

It behooves us to acknowledge yet another pitfall that has been discussed since the beginning of spiritual awareness. That is the concept of "evil", the dark side or negative force (embodied as Darth Vader in recent Lucas films). Darkness can operate as either a voice from within or a pull from without.

In our country today, and in the adult children of alcoholics movement, there is a spiritual awakening that is deeply exciting. More and more people are willing to "open up", to consider the existence of a power greater than themselves. Because of this there may be a naivete, a lack of discrimination about this larger dimension that can result in abuse. Indeed some teachings indicate that there is no need to discriminate, since everything is as it should be and all is unfolding perfectly. This, however, merely poses another paradox because thoughtful discrimination is advisable. For instance, we do not open the door of our house at any hour to any person who wishes to enter. It is naive to think that everyone "out there" is acting in a positive manner, and that there is no one who would use, abuse or hurt us. So we are careful. In other words, do your 100% *before* you turn it over.

There is a story of a cobra who was biting and killing the children of a small village. Finally the village elders went to the local guru and beseeched his help. The guru went to the snake and admonished him to stop biting the children. The snake humbly agreed. Shortly thereafter, the guru went on a pilgrimage. When he returned, he found the snake cowering under a rock, battered and bloodied.

"What happened to you?" exclaimed the guru.

The snake replied, "After the children discovered that I would no longer bite them, they began chasing me and stoning me every day. I am practically dead from their abuse!"

"You fool," said the guru. "I told you not to *bite* the children. I didn't tell you not to hiss!"

Similarly, it is an important part of being a parent to teach an appropriate guardedness to our children. We teach them that even those who look like they may just want to be helpful (i.e., the offer of a ride in a car) are to be evaluated first. And we teach them when and to whom we open the doors of our homes, helping them develop the judgment to live safely in our world. (Knowing who it is that is knocking and wanting to enter is the key to safety.) We also need to learn wisdom about when and to whom we open the doors of our inner self. The feeling of caution is a gift of wisdom, and unless it has become a problem, as it has in a disorder of paranoia, it is to be respected (Wayman, 1986).

We are also vulnerable to potential trouble from spiritual righteousness or arrogance. This is a very subtle trap. We can begin to feel like we have found the answers while others are still living in "the dark" or do not know what they are doing. We can also begin to believe that everything we feel or think comes from a spiritual center and therefore a higher source than others are using.

More than once we have heard, "We need to do it this way (i.e., *my* way) because that's what God wants." Remember, no one has a tie-line to God, and no one person has a monopoly on spiritual wisdom. Trust that others are doing their best, and know that sometimes our ego parades as spiritual guidance.

Other Pitfalls

In the *Bhagavad Gita,* an Eastern sacred book, which was written about 2500 years ago, we find the following warning:

> Three are the gates to this hell, the death of the soul: the gate of lust, the gate of wrath and the gate of greed. Let a man shun the three. When a man is free from these three doors of darkness, he does what is good for his soul, and then he enters the Path Supreme (16:21-22).

Of these three particular pitfalls, the most obvious stumbling block for children of alcoholics and other trauma is wrath. The anger, the resentment, the difficulty of forgiving our parents for their failings, and forgiving ourselves for not being perfect, make for a steep climb. In earlier stages of recovery it is important to acknowledge the existence of these feelings of anger about our parents in order to validate the trauma of childhood. In the stages of Genesis, forgiveness becomes part of the path. And because we are human, it needs to be achieved again and again.

Here we open our hearts to forgive our parents and invite gratitude for the gift of life. Here we are free to finally know the profoundness of the statement "They did the best they could being who they were" and respect can begin to grow. This does not mean that if our continued healing requires a distance from our parents that we must deny that. Rather it means that we are purging poison from our heart and purifying our soul.

Control may also become problematic in Genesis. The antidotes to control are surrender and detachment. We need to release our expectations of how life is to be, how Genesis is to be or where the path will lead us. Many turns in the road will be taken with little visibility, and require great faith that the universe is good, that there is a purpose for your life. When you run into a wall, it may just be God's way of saying "Take a right turn."

Remember that passage in the Christian scriptures about believing that if God will take such wonderful care of the lilies in the field and the birds in the air, you can know God will take wonderful care of you. Practice chunking it down (Gravitz & Bowden, 1985) in the same way you practiced in earlier stages: let go of a little control, or go forward on faith in just a small matter — not a huge decision like quitting your job and selling your house. Start with speaking up to a friend about something on your mind or trying a new church group. From the small, build to the larger decisions and issues.

Materialism

A more subtle and therefore more difficult obstacle is greed — or excessive materialism. At every turn we are surrounded by the consumer mentality and conspicuous consumption. The goal of all advertising is to increase our desire for a product. In fact, if an advertisement does not achieve that goal, it is replaced until one does. Affluence and luxury assail our senses constantly. And the nature of desire is usually to expand.

There dwells in America an often unspoken belief that wealth equals righteousness, poverty equals sloth or unrighteousness. A number of ministers promise affluence as a by-product of embracing their religious family with statements such as, "God never intended us to walk this earth in poverty. Riches are our inheritance. Open your arms to a generous God and He will fill them with plenty," as if the riches promised are mere material goods. Subtly the spiritual teaching of, "Go, sell all that you have and give to the poor" is transformed into, "If you have God's blessing, it will manifest in affluence." And some individuals have taken this idea the next step: "If you have little, you must not be a good (God-ly) person."

The authors do not believe that a good or God-ly life is closed to those who do not literally observe the command to give all possessions to the poor. The deeper, fuller meaning of this counsel refers to an inner psychological renunciation of external, material possessions so that we are not possessed by what we own. It means to let go of the need or desire for the possessions. Let them not be the foundation for your happiness or the reason for your actions. Free the conscious mind from possession by possessions. For those who choose to live in Genesis it is not enough to have a career, money in the bank, a Visa card and Calvin Klein underwear (Tamiazzo, 1986). Become increasingly aware that there is a reality of infinitely more value than the things you own or from which you derive social status (Yogananda, 1956).

To facilitate this awareness, make the connection with universal consciousness the number one goal. Make Genesis your priority. Become *willing* to let go of all you own should it interfere with that goal. Let the rule of advertising become your guide: "If this (whatever) doesn't get me to the goal, then I will change it until it does." Frequently question yourself about attachment to your possessions. Play with an image of yourself living in simplicity, without many of your current luxuries, with fewer items to take care of or be concerned about. Imagine yourself happy and fulfilled in a life where your home has simple furnishings which do not need to be oiled, covered or protected — where your principal activity consists of concerns about the spiritual path, rather than paying a host of bills and worrying about the things you need. Frequently ask, "Do I *really* need that?"

Consider the life of a Sadhu. The young men of India take a year before marriage and family to devote to living in poverty. With only a bowl for food, simple clothing and sandals, they journey across the land. They learn to live without and they learn to trust. This practice goes on even in the 20th century. Let yourself begin to know that your value is not related to how much money you have and what you own. Consider these words written of America almost a century ago:

> We have grown literally afraid to be poor. We despise anyone who elects to be poor in order to simplify and save his inner life . . . If he does not join the general scramble and pant with the money-making street, we deem him spiritless and lacking in ambition . . . Think of the strength which personal indifference to poverty would give us if we were devoted to unpopular causes . . . It is certain that the prevalent fear of poverty among the educated classes is the worst moral disease from which our civilization suffers (James, 1902).

So Who Am I?

Gerald Jampolsky makes an eloquent case that the one primary interference between God or love and us is fear (1970). We avoid Love for fear of vulnerability, for fear of rejection, for fear of loss. We avoid living our lives for and in God, for fear of being ridiculed, being rejected or being poor. In Genesis there is a leap of faith and a building of the vision that the Supreme Power is good. The primary issue is learning to live on a higher path from a center of love.

The Delphic Oracle's admonition to "Know Thyself" is part of this challenge. It takes great courage to see the face of God (Higher Power/Universal Consciousness). Before you gaze upon the face of God, you must look at all the things that are within you, all things that are part of you. You must look within, see past all the illusions and the glamour to the reality of who you are. You must see the God within yourself and the God within all others. You must see your potential for good and your potential for bad. Then you will see God (John-Roger, 1985).

A scene in a 1980s movie, *"The Never Ending Story"*, shows the hero going through numerous trials to get to the Oracle, a mysterious and magical being. The final trial is to look into a mirror and see himself, see himself fully. No one before this boy had survived this "knowing" of himself. Imagine looking into a mirror and seeing all your flaws, all your weaknesses, all the areas you handle poorly! *And* seeing all your strengths and goodness. The previous five stages of recovery, when taken over time, provide such a mirror, and provide the foundation of health which allows one to look — to look and accept.

Again, this type of commitment occurs late in recovery so that adult children have built faith in themselves and have established a reliable support system. To leap into the Genesis stage too early in recovery may lead to another self-abandonment, an escapist focus on others and a harsh, judgmental non-acceptance of your imperfection, rather than a joyful effort of a God-like life.

The Price of Love

One other pitfall needs to be considered. It is the price of love. To live in Genesis is to increase in love, to expand who and what we love. Everything has a price, even love. To love and be concerned about a wider and wider group of people is to embrace the cares of the world. But the price for what we get in return is worth paying. And the cost for not loving is too high to even consider.

The price of love can be the pain parents feel when their child has an accident or dies. If we did not love that person, we could feel insensitive just as we do when we read of a killing in another country. But if we love, then the pain pierces our hearts. And the further we go into Genesis, the more we love and, therefore, the more we become vulnerable.

To truly love on the human plane is to foster freedom in the loved one. To truly love on the spiritual plane is to value God's choices even when they differ from ours.

A Light Heart

It is important to make this journey with a light heart. Paradoxically, even while expanding the concerns of the heart, we expand our faith and peace. So do not have a timetable and do not view this as a somber, joyless duty. Rather, acknowledge that the timetable is not yours to calculate. This search is destined to fill you with lightness and life beyond your imagining. A prayer that summarizes these thoughts is:

> *God, grant me the patience to allow your will to unfold according to* your *wishes and timetable;*
> *Grant me the wisdom to recognize your will;*
> *And grant me the willingness and courage to act upon it. Thank you (Bowden, 1986).*

9

How Can A Person Identify Genesis Experiences?

The real voyage of discovery consists not in seeking new landscapes but in having new eyes (Proust, 1920).

The Un-nameable

Spirituality is not intellectually "know-able". It is only "be-able" (Whitfield, 1985). We can only provide a map — and a vague one at that — with the reminder that the map is not the territory, and that to label this profound experience is to move away from it.

An ancient proverb states, "He who knows does not speak, and he who speaks does not know." So read this mindful of that. This is only a map of the journey, not the destination. Earlier we mentioned that rituals are not the lesson or the goal, they are only techniques to attain awareness of the universal. The menu is not the meal.

There are two primary ways to identify if you are living your own spiritual truths and if you are living a Genesis

lifestyle. One is in the fruit of your actions; the other is in
how you feel.

A powerful guide for recognition has been presented in
the Christian scriptures: ". . . are grapes gathered from
thorns, or figs from thistles? So, every sound tree bears good
fruit, but the bad tree bears evil fruit . . . thus you will know
them by their fruits" (Mat. 7:16-20). Whether it be your own
experience or another's, look at the effects. Does it bring
peace? Does it cause harm? By your fruits shall ye be known.

This is meant as a guidance to observe the outcome of
your actions (or the results of others' actions) and see if they
produce good in the world and good for others. Look at how
people feel after they have been in contact with you. Do
they feel better or do they feel worse? Are you increasing the
positive energy on the planet or leaving behind you
negative energy? Observe what effect you are having, and
adjust your behavior accordingly.

This is not an all-or-none issue. People living a spiritual
life still voice anger or displeasure, still have confrontations
and occasionally have a bad day. As a general rule of thumb,
however, living a spiritual life benefits all who come in
contact with you. It enhances every activity and increases the
chance of success.

This is also known as "steering by the wake". Adjustments
in direction are made according to the pattern of the wake
or water behind the moving boat. As you steer a boat
through water, a path is left where the boat has cut through
the water's surface. To steer by the wake, you check the
water behind the boat to see if it flows in a straight line or
if the wake is curved. If the water disturbance is curved and
you intend to go straight ahead, you correct your steering
according to the direction and degree of the curve until the
path is straight.

Diversity

It is helpful to read what others have said about the
spiritual life. Descriptions of expanded consciousness

experiences can be found in such diverse literature as *The Talmud, The Holy Bible* and *The Bhagavad Gita.* They are also described by such writers as William James and Aldous Huxley, as well as East Indian writings and such places as the Harvard Center for Research in Personality. Most people, of course, are used to ordinary, waking states of consciousness. Our less frequent states are typically referred to as "alternate" or "altered" states of consciousness and include daydreams, sleep, dreams, trance states, drug intoxication or peak experiences, among others (Tart, 1975).

A second key to identifiying Genesis experiences is in how your life feels to you. Throughout the ages and throughout the literature, experiences in Genesis are commonly characterized by a feeling of unity with self, others and the universe, as well as moments of calmness, strength, courage and a still quiet inner certainty.

Even though peacefulness is usually associated with a spiritual life, it is not usually a constant characteristic of Genesis. Again, there is the story of Bill W. and his "winter of discontent". In the midst of his struggle, Father Ed arrived at his doorstep. After hours of sharing, Bill asked Father Ed if he would ever be fully at peace. As Bill wrestled with anger, impatience and dissatisfaction, Father Ed advised him that a person growing in spirituality is distinguished by yearning, restlessness and "thirst". Father Ed called it "divine dissatisfaction" (Thomsen, 1975).

As described by Phoebe in *The House Of the Green Gables,* "The world owes all its forward movement to men of dissatisfaction" (Hawthorne, 1950). Again, a paradox exists. As we learn to stay focused on larger and more positive aspects of the universe, such as love, God or cosmic consciousness, there is an increasing peacefulness within, yet we are called to ever greater challenges.

Awakenings

Awakening or expanded consciousness occurs with glimpses that "things" or "reality" are not the way we thought they were. Similar to the precipitant of the second stage of recovery, Emergent Awareness (Gravitz & Bowden, 1985), something breaks into our old way of thinking with a new possibility. Our every day, fixed beliefs and ideas are conditioned by our history, language, culture, race and gender, among other things. Release from these limitations allows fragmented awareness to meld into universality. It allows Genesis! Bill W.'s awakening has been described as follows:

> He suddenly seemed caught up in a kind of joy, an ecstasy such as he would never find words to describe. It was as though he were standing high on a mountaintop and a strong clear wind blew against him, around him, through him but it seemed a wind not of air, but of spirit and as this happened, he had the feeling that he was stepping into another world, a new world of consciousness, and everywhere now there was a wonderous feeling of Presence which all his life he had been seeking (Thomsen, 1975).

Bill never again doubted the existence of a Higher Power. Nor did he drink again. When a Genesis experience is this dramatic, there is little doubt in identification. However, most of our lives are filled with "small miracles", easy to ignore or explain away. You may recall events in your own life that at the time you knew to be extraordinary — impossible except for the existence of a Higher Power. Yet it is likely that those memories have slipped into obscurity, no longer providing the awe of recognition of God. You might want to take time now to remember those experiences.

Synchronicity

The perspective of Genesis would include recognizing the concept of synchronicity, of learning what physicists have been learning: all things are connected. The next step would be to take a leap of faith that the energy making up everything is positive and deliberately arranges "coincidences" for your higher good.

For instance, it is possible to consider that this book was *purposefully* (i.e., cosmically) delivered into your possession — that you are reading it because right now is exactly the right time for you to learn about this material.

One of Bill W.'s favorite sayings was, "When the pupil is ready, the teacher appears." Whitfield adds, "And when the pupil is *not* ready, teachers still appear — we just don't recognize them" (1986). Consider the possibilities.

Living Genesis is truly done one day at a time and, sometimes, one moment at a time. This is where the AA slogan, "one day at a time", becomes an integral practice — live each day as your one, your only, your last. Live each day as though it is the final opportunity you will have to glorify the best a human can be. The more you can keep this perspective, the richer life becomes. It is similar to the attitude people often have while traveling in a foreign country. "I may never pass this way again."

A loved one on a recent trip to India found that life changed in a profound way when she greeted each morning as part of an unfolding adventure. The waiter at breakfast suddenly becomes a family that needs clothing sent from the United States; the man stranded at the airport becomes her host that evening; the couple in the taxi with a flat tire later become escorts on a pilgrimage through the streets of Varanasi to the Ganges River; the "randomly chosen" taxi cab driver has first-hand information on the friend who was mysteriously missing at the airport that morning in another city.

Recently, at a gas station, the same person mentioned her trip to India and wound up being driven to a local ashram to meet a teacher. That teacher later provided one of the quotes for this book. Another time, stopping to help two stranded motorists, one ended up by offering a service which was needed that very night.

Another example occurred in one of our psychotherapy groups. A young woman had decided to work on a very difficult and frightening issue. In order to facilitate her work, we had arranged with her that when she was ready to work, she would invite us to sit next to her for support. The invitation itself was meaningful work because she had been trained by her alcoholic father to never ask for help on anything — it was considered a sign of weakness. That night as we all filed into the group room, the man who normally sat next to her stopped, turned to the therapist who was going to be the physical support, and said, "May I switch seats with you tonight? I'd like to sit in your chair."

The same wonders can occur in our own daily environment, although it requires frequent refocusing away from our normal, daily concerns and towards the expanded view of Genesis.

Synchronicity appears to increasingly occur in the stage of Genesis as we begin to perceive the universe in the context of a Higher Power. Coincidences that are so amazing as to defy rational thought come to our attention. Because most of us unconsciously screen our experiences according to what we believe to be possible or real, we often do not "notice" synchronistic events.

10

What Can I Do To Cultivate The Perspective, Experience And Lifestyle Of Genesis?

Until one is committed, there is hesitancy, the chance to draw away, ineffectiveness. Concerning all acts of initiative (and creation), there is one elementary truth, the ignorance of which kills countless ideas and splendid plans: that the moment one definitely commits oneself, then Providence moves, too. All sorts of things occur to help one that would otherwise never have occurred. A whole stream of events issues from the decision, raising in one's favor all manner of unforeseen incidents and meetings and material assistance, which no man could have dreamed would have come his way. Whatever you can do, or dream you can, begin it. Boldness has genius, power and magic in it. Begin it now! (Goethe, 1902).

God As The Goal

There are many routes to living Genesis, perceiving Genesis and experiencing Genesis. The lifestyle is built day by day through living the Golden Rule. In general, the best direction can be gained by acquainting yourself with the lives of saints of all ages and all religions. Study their lives. Learn how they conducted themselves. A perceptual shift can result from a variety of factors, from reading this book, from studying spiritual literature, from having an emotional spiritual experience, from the minute changes that occur as you daily live a spiritual lifestyle. The emotional experience can be induced through guided imagery, or the event of a miracle occurring in your life that takes your breath away and leaves your heart filled with wonder.

There also exists the paradox that while you can and should prepare yourself for a spiritual life, you cannot control the actual experience of "enlightenment". What is needed are paths to penetrate the plane of the relative and enter the plane of the absolute, coupled with a faith that your awareness of that greater plane will come when it is right, not when you decide.

From a spiritual perspective there is no competition among the roads leading to Genesis. Many are the paths, but one is the Truth. You have already started on one path by reading this book. Two central principles in behavior lead to the Genesis lifestyle. The first is to seek it ardently. This is described in much of the literature as loving God above all else. The second is to embrace the Biblical directive: "Love thy neighbor as thyself."

We have been told, "Seek and ye shall find". Dare to have faith that this is true, and dare to open your eyes, your ears and your heart a little wider to recognize teachings from all around you. As the *Talmud* states, "It matters not whether you do much or little, so long as your heart is directed toward heaven."

There have been teachers and guides to higher conscious-ness down through the ages. From the Sermon on the Mount delivered by Jesus of Nazareth almost 2,000 years ago comes this directive for attaining a Genesis life and perspective: "Blessed are they which do hunger and thirst for righteousness; for they shall be filled". Or there is the Hassidic saying, "Do you know where the Lord is to be found? He is in the place where He is invited to enter." You may want to take a moment here and appreciate how far you have already traveled, and recognize the resources you have already discovered. Resources and teachers are not limited to human form. Reading this far is a reflection of your commitment.

There is a story of a disciple who asked his teacher how he could realize God. "Come along," said the teacher. "I will show you." He took the disciple to a lake and both stepped in. Suddenly the teacher reached over and pressed the disciple's head under water. A few minutes later he released him and asked: "Well, how did you feel?" "Oh, I was dying for a breath of air!" gasped the disciple. Then the teacher said: "When you feel that intensely for God, you won't have to wait long for his vision" (Prabhavananda, 1963).

Teachings of all ages and all cultures describe the deep and sincere longing for higher consciousness as the path "Home". This intense dedication is tenderly stated in the following words:

"One thing I am left with, no doubt whatsoever, — God exists. In a very personal as well as impersonal way. And He loves us more than we can fathom. And if we will only continually seek Him out, in love (not anger or blame or pain), He will always be there for us. Always. Never doubt that, my friend. Cry no more. For our eternal friend has you safely, as long as you lift your arms to the Light. If you will only rejoice in your love for one another, He cannot let you down . . . (Loved One, 1986)

Love Thy Neighbor

The directive to love thy neighbor as thyself belongs in all three aspects of Genesis: as a perception, an emotional experience and a lifestyle. Perceptually, we must learn to view all others as our family, as connected to us. We need to see that we are all in the same boat, breathing the same air and are made of the same elements. Emotionally, love needs to resonate inside us as we interact with our fellow beings. Love is the appropriate response to "our neighbors", even if we disapprove of their behavior, or their looks or whatever. We can still voice our differences within the context of that love. And with the lifestyle of Genesis, that love would be acted out in the ways we treat one another. We would be thoughtful, generous, compassionate. We would help others when we are able to help. We would value human life above material goods and act on those values.

Detachment

To make an ongoing recovery in Genesis, the priority invariably includes a detachment from material longings. Detachment is a way to recover from the adverse effects of living with someone who has the disease of alcoholism or other chemical dependence. It is neither kind nor unkind and does not imply evaluation of the person or things from which we are detaching. Rather, we detach from the agony of the involvement.

Detachment as a cure for suffering is fundamental to Hinduism and is one of the Four Noble Truths central to Buddhism:

1) Life is suffering
2) Suffering is due to desire/attachments
3) The path to happiness is to attain Nirvana or to tune one's self to God
4) The method is the Noble Eightfold Path.

The Eightfold Path includes right views (acceptance of Buddha's teachings); right thoughts (positive thinking); right speech; right conduct; right livelihood; right effort (seek, expend energy); right mindfulness (maintain awareness of the truth); and right concentration (appropriate spiritual exercises). The Eightfold Path is a profound and thorough teaching used by many to guide themselves on the path to a better life.

Detachment involves letting go of one's expectations and becoming aware that possession of material goods never brings lasting satisfaction. Teresa of Avila believed surrender was one of the three practices helpful in communicating with one's Higher Power, the other two being love and faith (Teresa of Avila, 1980).

There is a story about a man whose horse ran away. His neighbors came to him saying, "What a shame. Your horse has run away. This is very bad luck." All the man replied was, "Perhaps." The next day his horse returned with several wild horses in tow. His neighbors came over to congratulate him on his good luck. "Perhaps," he responded. The following week his son broke his leg trying to ride one of the wild horses. The neighbors came over to commiserate with him. "Those wild horses weren't such good luck after all," they said. "Perhaps," the man replied. Not long afterwards, war broke out with a neighboring country. The army came through and recruited all the young, able-bodied men to fight. The man's son was passed by because of his broken leg. This time the neighbors came saying, "Oh, what good luck for your son to have broken his leg." "Perhaps," said the man. And so life goes.

Accepting what is and letting go are part of detachment, surrender and relinquishing control. Happiness is a function of joyfully accepting what is without adding or subtracting anything from it. Alcoholics Anonymous has slogans which address acceptance and surrender such as: "Let go and let God", "Easy does it", "Live and let live" and "Turn it over."

Control is a Core Issue for children of alcoholics (Gravitz & Bowden, 1985) and must be surrendered bit by bit, step by step. Life felt so out of control during childhood that we learned to hold on to control as a survival strategy. When it is time to turn our lives over to a power greater than ourselves, it can be frightening. We think we turned it over only to discover we bargained. We think we turned it over only to discover new levels of surrender before us. Take your time with this issue and know it does not have to be done with an all-or-none approach.

New Perception

The ability to detach and accept *what is* ushers in the unification of the mind, body and spirit. The subtle exploration into the obvious is a major part of the awakening process. While full mastery may be elusive, partial mastery can begin right now. Only the old, worn filters of the mind prevent us from perceiving the staggering beauty of our completeness and the incredible unfolding around us. You can, however, expect the unexpected. Guidance will be provided from unimagined sources.

There are some simple steps to help us alter our limited view of the world. One strategy to recognize experiences through expanded vision is as follows:

1) Begin to question whether there is more to experience in any given moment than you first realize
2) Given these first glimpses, conceive that there *may* be more
3) Continue to experience and note these moments
4) While experiencing all of these, conceive there are still more
5) Repeat this same cycle over and over again (Joy, 1982).

This kind of daily training is also outlined in *A Course in Miracles*, (1975) with groups throughout the country meeting to practice the lessons.

A complementary strategy is the Zen Buddhist concept of the "beginner's mind". The beginner's mind is that state of consciousness which is open, receptive, unencumbered and completely available, so that all things are experienced as if for the first time. It is when we know that we do not know, and we are fully willing to learn. It is like when we visit a new culture or start learning a new language. In the beginner's mind it is as if nothing has ever been experienced before and everything is totally new. The attempt is made to bypass the everyday filters of the mind, yet to do so without naivete. So to use this strategy we would consciously decide to approach a situation with the beginner's mind.

For an extensive description of spiritual recovery, we recommend *Alcoholism, Other Drug Problems, and Spirituality: Stress Management and Serenity During Recovery,* by Charles Whitfield (1985). Whitfield describes a series of guiding principles. The first is living in the here and now, analogous to the concept of the beginner's mind. Living in the here and now is difficult because our minds are unruly and often preoccupied with the past and future. What is guilt but living in the past? What is anxiety but living in the future? Children of alcoholics enter adulthood with much of our energy tied up in the trauma we have experienced. It takes a great deal of our current energy to hold back a great deal of our past pain, leaving little energy for the present (Cermak, 1985). To enter deeply into this present moment is to become immersed into eternity. Living in the present characterizes peak experiences.

Positive Thinking

Positive thinking is viewing our life as an integral and productive part of the "cosmic drama" and involves many of the spiritual practices already discussed, including surrender, viewing the bad that befalls us as a gift and working to detach from life's dance of melodrama. To achieve positive thinking or an "attitude of gratitude", we must select our friends wisely. Yogananda stated,"Environment is greater than will" (1956). It is important to remember that and spend time with people who support our efforts to create thoughts that make us happy.

Adult children of alcoholics or trauma think negatively or speak to themselves with a critical internal voice. In fact, if we received a phone call and the voice on the other end of the line spoke to us the way we speak to ourselves, we would consider it an obscene phone call and hang up! Thinking positively involves redirecting the mind from the habitual, negative thoughts to a new pattern. Just like any unused muscle, it takes time to build strength up so that positive thoughts are the norm and become habitual. Much of this work will have been accomplished in the earlier stages of recovery. However, there is a tendency to return to the old familiar pattern of thinking or speaking, so the change requires conscious effort and practice while the new pattern is being learned. And even afterwards, we need to be mindful of our vulnerability to self-criticism.

The physician that helped Bill W. back to life, Dr. Silkworth, believed alcoholism was best treated by directing the alcoholic away from any deep or morbid examination of the past. This is usually true for chemical sobriety. This same treatment is helpful for adult children of alcoholics and children of other trauma in the recovery stage of Genesis. Fully letting go of the past belongs here, *after* the examination, illumination and reexperiencing. Only after the secret pain has been validated and grieved can it be released. That is the path to emotional sobriety.

Quiet the Noise

Another change we believe you will need to consciously include for your spiritual development is a method to quiet the noise in your life and in your mind.

The world is filled with noise and distractions, from television to social chatter to unbidden thoughts. It will become increasingly important for you to develop a process of turning off the external noise and tuning in the internal voice — that still, quiet voice within. There is no one right way to do this. You might find that setting aside time at sunset to watch the earth's rotation away from the light source, to watch the changing colors, to feel the changing atmosphere, to hear the sounds at dusk and breathe in tune with the experience will take you right into that special quiet place inside where you commune with that which is holy. Or you might set up an altar in your own home for formal meditation/prayer time. Whatever method you choose, it is important to actively seek the "inactive" moment of communion.

Meditation

Meditation or contemplative prayer is a crucial spiritual practice for cultivating the Genesis perspective experience and lifestyle, and one we find particularly fruitful. Bill W. conceptualized it as listening during prayer (Thomsen, 1975).

There are many methods taught to achieve a quiet, meditative state. It is the process of learning to penetrate the subtle strata of consciousness and enlarge our context of reality (Fishel, 1987). It quiets the mind and opens the heart (Whitfield, 1985; Muktananda, 1981). Meditation provides a source of potential energy and intelligence within us all. By becoming still, quiet and meditative, we can listen to our inner voice, the Higher Self, more clearly. Silence allows the truth to become manifest.

There is a story of a man who was praying fervently for guidance on a specific problem he had. For weeks he had implored God for help with no response. One day, in frustration, he ended his prayer by saying angrily, "Why don't you say something?!" Finally, God's voice was heard: "I can't get a word in edgewise!"

Discussions of this "listening" technique can be found in the oldest records of human experience, *The Vedas*. Simply praying sincerely or asking for help can be the spark that ignites a Genesis experience. Bill W.'s spiritual awakening was precipitated by his desperate plea, "Oh God. If there is a God, show me. Give me some sign" (Thomsen, 1975).

Guide to Meditation

Some simple guides for meditating are:

1) Find a quiet, peaceful place where you can be alone for 10 to 20 minutes without interruption
2) Sit comfortably with a straight back on a chair or cushion
3) Take five minutes to read or listen to something spiritually uplifting and inwardly calming
4) Close your eyes and breathe deeply and slowly
5) Focus your attention on a passage or word you have read, or on your breath
6) When your attention wanders, gently bring it back
7) Continue as long as is comfortable
8) End with a prayer
9) Write down whatever you want to remember and take it with you wherever you go during the day (Tamiazzo, 1986).

Meditation is only one of a number of altered states of consciousness that allows us to transcend our ordinary waking consciousness. Suspending our beliefs permits us to be much more open to our experience, enabling us to learn more about ourselves, others and the universe through direct experience, which is our best teacher.

For example, firewalking is increasingly included in growth seminars for just this purpose. If all your life you have held a belief that walking on red glowing coals will burn your feet to a crisp and then you participate in a firewalk where you walk on coals exceeding 1200 degrees Fahrenheit without even a blister, you will never again be able to return to your old belief. It is an indelible impression. Expose yourself to experiences that push the frontiers of your beliefs and realities, while keeping in mind the primary goal of spirituality.

Suspending our beliefs is intimately connected to another spiritual practice: using our imagination. When we imagine something, we can transcend countless barriers. There is an old saying, "Where the mind has been, the body can go." A statement often heard in self-help programs is, "If you don't believe, make believe." Therapists may use guided imagery or directed imagination as a tool for healing, for expansion and for going beyond current limitations.

Additional spiritual practices include:

1) Being humble, which involves being open, listening, and nondefensiveness while being honest with ourself and others
2) Accepting our shadow or darker side
3) Being responsible or transcending victimization by taking responsibility for our life
4) Working a program like Alcoholics Anonymous or Al-Anon
5) Helping others (Whitfield, 1985).

A daily commitment is important, perhaps essential, to progress on this road. Genesis includes a commitment of faith and trust in a power greater than ourself, as well as a commitment to the community of humanity, not just once, but over and over. Do not let laziness or loss of faith stop your spiritual progress. As we have said, Genesis is lived one day at a time and sometimes one moment at a time. It requires us to fight attachments, fear, loss of faith and loss of energy in order to wage a war of love.

As you grow in Genesis, you may find this prayer by Saint Francis of Assisi a useful guide:

Lord make me an instrument of thy peace.
Where there is hatred, let me sow love;
Where there is injury, pardon;
Where there is doubt, faith;
Where there is despair, hope;
Where there is darkness, light;
Where there is sadness, joy.
O divine Master, grant that I may not so much seek
To be consoled as to console,
To be understood as to understand
To be loved as to love:
For it is in giving that we receive,
It is in pardoning that we are pardoned,
It is in dying to self that we are born to eternal life.

(Cited in Easwaran, 1984)

11

Can You Provide A Concrete Example Of How A Genesis Or Spiritual Experience Can Be Induced?

The Desert Fathers did not think of solitude as being alone, but as being alone with God. They did not think of silence as not speaking but as listening to God (Henri Nouwen, 1973).

The Genesis Journey

Historically, both a perceptual shift (expanded awareness or consciousness) and an emotional recognition have been attained momentarily through a variety of techniques, including the use of drugs, food or sleep deprivation, prolonged periods of meditation or prayer, or total surrender to help such as Bill W. experienced. For a simple exercise to practice at home, you can tape record the following and play it back to yourself as many times as you find it useful. We can be the stimulus; you are the response.

First, make yourself physically comfortable. Take a moment to get acquainted with the chair in which you are sitting. Feel its support against your back. Feel its support under your thighs. Feel your feet resting comfortably on the floor. Become aware of your body and, as you do, you can begin to enjoy knowing that there is nothing you really have to do for the next few minutes. You don't have to say anything. You don't have to be anything. You don't even have to listen fully with all of your conscious awareness.

You might even enjoy discovering that your eyes can close. And as they do, you may notice how rhythmic, how even and how deep your breathing is becoming. Feel your chest expand and contract, go in and out, and as you allow yourself to discover how very comfortable you can become, you can allow your mind to just drift and wander. As you continue to sit there more and more comfortably, aware of the air entering and leaving your lungs, begin to let go of these surroundings as if the chair and room and these words are fading.

Let a picture of yourself or a sense of yourself begin to form. Slowly and comfortably let that sense or image be part of your awareness. Be with that awareness for a moment. Now begin to imagine a sphere of light and joy surrounding you, emanating from your body. Feel its lightness, sense its lightness.

Next begin to realize, to sense that you are going on a journey, a cosmic journey. You might float up in the sphere of light and joy, floating up, up.

Notice the room below you. Float still higher and see, sense the building down below. Now see the street, the block, then the city as you travel upward. Now you can see or sense the state, and greater parts of the country stretching out below you. As you continue moving farther into the universe, imagine other countries and now the entire earth below you.

Now our solar system, and now the Milky Way, and now just stars everywhere, earth's sun blending into all the other suns.

Become aware of a doorway or a clearing or a space. Imagine walking through a door or seeing through a clearing. There could be the presence of a powerful, loving energy or light. Commune with that great force; dialogue with that energy. Ask for guidance in your search or in your experience of Genesis. Whether words, feelings, or pictures come to you, take the time to pause. Let this positive energy just slowly come to you, even if it is not yet clear, or seems to be vague. Take a few moments now as you sit quietly to listen, to become more deeply aware of this higher self, to become more familiar with yourself as you are in this space . . . comfortable, calm, loved.

Next, and at your own pace, begin to return to the Milky Way, and now our solar system. As you continue back, you can become aware of the earth, the country, the state, the city, the block, the street, this building, this room, and this chair. Become more and more aware of your surroundings, bringing back with you the comfort and awareness of this experience. And when you are ready, allow your eyes to open, becoming fully present, feeling alert, refreshed, clear-headed and relaxed all over.

There are as many responses to this experience as there are experiencers. All are important; all are real. Some may enjoy the comfort; some may enjoy what they discovered. One woman who did this exercise in a workshop with us reported that when she returned to the room, her Higher Power returned with her and was there beside her as she spoke to us.

Again, there is no one "right" way to live Genesis. As you consider the various parts of this book, ask yourself what rang most true or most appropriate for you? Your answers to that question are the most appropriate directions for you.

12

Diane's Story

*Come to a limit and transcend it. Our only
security lies in our ability to change (John Lilly,
1984).*

Joyful and Difficult

Feelings of joy and peace will gradually increase. You will
experience less and less that old feeling of wondering what
the point is, of feeling empty and useless. More and more
you will find a reason for living. It is likely that friends, old
and new, will comment on how even tempered you seem to
be emotionally. You will recall when you used to live on a
roller coaster. The new feeling is often referred to as "being
centered". Your feet are under you, your eyes are clear and
your step is more confident. Living in the stage of Genesis
has no limits, and holds promise of untold riches. And you
truly must do the work of the first five stages before Genesis
will work for you.

It is also true that the spiritual quest is a journey of ups
and downs. As we have stated, it is not one of clear, step-by-
step, upward progress. Doubts and fears will continue to

assail you. You will get sidetracked or "duped" by false teachers and well-meaning friends. You will lose hope and forget the progress you have made. You will tire and despair of ever really "arriving".

And the "highs" do not last forever. In fact, the phenomena of visions, lights, dreams or voices are not necessarily a hallmark of spiritual progress. They may or may not come, and even if they do, they are not a basis for judging one's progress. *The degree of peace, calm, joy, detachment and unconditional love in one's life is the basis of an increasingly spiritual life.*

You will experience a new balance of positive feelings. Where once you may have felt good only a quarter of a time, now you will feel bad only a quarter of the time. Three quarters of the time you will feel the joy and the peace of living at a higher level of consciousness.

The secret of success in Genesis is to *always* continue to strive for spiritual awakening, to free yourself from the doubts and trauma of the past, to clear your eyes for the present and to keep them there, firm in the knowledge that this is a new life born from the old. And nothing, but nothing, will turn you back (Wilcove, 1986). For even in Genesis, success continues to be getting up one more time than you fall down.

One picture is worth a thousand words, and metaphors can illuminate paths otherwise not clearly seen. We invite you to share Diane's story, a composite of many people's journey.

Diane's Story

Tears came to Diane's eyes when she heard Fred's words.

"Scared. I'm scared," she whispered silently to herself, beginning to sense that old familiar blankness in her mind.

"I've come so far. I've worked so hard. I've made so many changes and become so much happier. Why am I crying at his words? Why do they scare me so much?" These were all the thoughts going through her mind. For sitting across from her this day, years into her recovery, Diane's friend Fred had said "Now you can stop identifying yourself as the child of an alcoholic."

It had been years since Diane first began to acknowledge that she was the child of an alcoholic and experience the panic, relief, shame and guilt that followed, and had begun the halting journey into recovery.

It seemed then that her creation had been followed by a fall. As a child she learned hard lessons. For years she had lived in the unpredictable chaos that is the hallmark of the alcoholic family. At last as an adult came Emergent Awareness and the flooding of emotions and memories. The tyrannical chains binding her as an adult child to those once-useful, but now dysfunctional ways of responding to the world dropped away. What relief! How overwhelming! She struggled through the Core Issues. A multitude of situations called up the automatic survival functioning, but allowed another change, another transformation, another opportunity to increase the strength of her new responses.

She went into therapy — not just once, but several times over several years, as difficult situations once again revived childhood memories of pain, confusion and anger. New friends offered encouragement and support as she slowly progressed, sometimes two steps forward and one step back. They were there for the crisis calls, her sobbing into the phone that there was no hope, things would never be better, there was no reason to pretend she could possibly change. They had listened to her, heard her, reassured her that she would come through and that reaching out with a phone call was welcomed healthy behavior. They were there when she was overwhelmed and confused in a new relationship — unable to tolerate the ambiguity of a healthy man who did not come to her needy and dependent, interpreting his independence as a lack of love.

Again and again Diane had gathered her energy and reinvested in herself and her personal growth, determined that this time she would not abandon herself to the old patterns etched so deeply and so early.

And life had indeed changed. As her views and her beliefs changed, the world around her had become welcoming, warm, filled with opportunity, instead of danger and isolation. And finally, in Integration, there was the joining together of her fragmented selves into a harmonious whole; her thoughts, feelings, and actions finally reflecting a unified person whose existence was primarily free of the childhood pain.

Yet these few simple words spoken by Fred brought the tears, the fears, the denial: "Now can you stop being the child of an alcoholic? Can you stop being damaged?"

If Fred were anyone but a trusted friend, she would reject the suggestion immediately, just as she had early in her recovery when acquaintances and family members had accused her of dredging up the past to place blame on her parents and evade personal responsibility for her life. She had forced herself to go forward on the journey and through the exploration without their support.

There was something different about it this time. It was not an accusation, but an invitation.

"You exist. What other proof of your worth can match 'the gift of life'? You are okay just as you are, without having to prove it."

Diane's own voice whispered inside her as he spoke, questioning his words: "Am I enough? Am I really all right? Can I stop the struggle?" The fear welled inside.

Fred's voice broke through again. "Diane, you don't need to be married, you don't need to work an 80-hour week, you don't need to show others how well you're doing. You are a valuable person just as you are, even though you make mistakes, even though you get scared hearing me, even though sometimes you don't recognize yourself as being okay. Now that you are reconnected to yourself, you can trust yourself and your resources."

Fred then told her the Zen story of the disciple going to his master for enlightenment. The master asked, "What is the answer to life? Go and seek."

The disciple searched for three years, then returned saying, "Master, I have the answer."

"What is it?" the master asked. The disciple replied, "It is this," and described his discovery.

The master replied, "No. Go again and seek."

Another three years went by and the disciple returned. "Master, I have the answer."

"What is it?" "It is this," said the disciple describing new discoveries.

"No! Go again and seek."

For 15 years this continued until finally the disciple returned saying, "Master, at last I have the answer to life . . . there is no question!"

Diane felt confused. She wasn't sure what he meant. Yet a shock of recognition and truth reverberated within her.

Then words from a therapist she had seen during her recovery came to mind: "Only with confusion can there be openness to searching. Only with that time of confusion can an old way die. And only then can a new way be born."

She remembered a woman in group psychotherapy describe her fear of change by saying she felt like she was in a large swimming pool, holding onto the side, knowing she had to let go and swim out to the center, even though she wasn't certain she could do it. Diane now understood the sinking feeling, the fear that she would be without support, with nothing to hold on to.

And then the therapist's response to the woman's fear came to her mind, "Check out all the sides of the pool carefully. Let go with just one hand at first. Next swim out just a few feet. Then return to the side. Take it slowly. Take it in stages."

It had been so difficult to take it in stages and believe she could recover. As a child she had undertaken the impossible task of being her own parent. It had fostered a deep sense of inadequacy and a desperate desire for someone to take care of her. But it was also true that she really did perform that child's impossible task — she survived.

"You will be okay just as you are. You have all that is needed. You are more than you think you are," Fred added.

Diane glanced up, catching her image in a mirror. Again her therapist's words came to her. "Look at yourself. Say 'Thank you' to yourself for having such amazing determination and for getting yourself here. Say 'Thank you' to yourself for having the strength and courage to go on." She smiled a thank you at her reflection. Fred's words became a comfort, no longer calling forth fear. She began to realize it really was time to go on. There were other places to go, other things to do. And she could do it.

As Diane stepped outside, she was struck by the brightness of the light. Looking around, she became acutely aware of the sky's blueness, the power of the mountains, the many aspects of her surroundings. She caught sight of tiny, translucent green shoots pushing their way through the earth's crust. Another winter was yielding to spring. And with quiet amazement she again felt tears in her eyes.

"I make a difference. Life, death, this planet . . . we do make a difference. When I as one person illuminate my life, and clarify my history, it affects the light and clarity of the world."

She imagined herself running on wet sand at surf's edge. Each step left an impression in the sand. The waves rolled up the shore, outlining a new pattern, dipping into the trace of her footprint. As the wave receded, it splashed up the edges of the print, again reshaping its course. Wave after wave washed over it until the footprint was obliterated, no longer visible to the eye. She wondered, "Is it possible to consider that those few moments in the ocean's history had changed its path forever in some way, had indelibly affected it?" No longer was she merely a separate, unrelated being, but an integral part of history. She sensed her own participation in the ancient evolution of the human race.

She knew she would forget this moment. She also knew that just as before, the forgetting would be another opportunity and impetus for her to make another even stronger connection. Deep within she was aware that her "goodbye" to being a "child of an alcoholic" was indeed the "welcome" to a new beginning. There was a comforting awareness of traveling the road alone, yet an accompanying awareness that in her individuality she was connected to everything.

Diane sensed that this path on the journey required a renewed effort, demanded the recommitment of energy and a new kind of courage — much different from that required by the initial stages of recovery. There was no map and there was no certainty that her life, her actions, were of and for the greater whole. She must act on faith. Now she must have spiritual courage.

Dawn's light began to flood the landscape that had been previously shrouded in shadows, half-lights and darkness. Hope emerged. Diane walked forward with a new awareness. She walked in the light of her own spirit. Diane had survived. She was emerging into another level of awareness (Barnabei, 1982).

And so the journey continues. It goes on and on as you get better and better, "weller than well", as is said in AA.

Epilogue

What we call the beginning is often the end and to make an end is to make a beginning. The end is where we start from (T.S. Eliot, 1940).

As much as we have been able to say about Genesis, in the end we are still left with the realization of its paradoxical and mysterious nature. Yet once we accept the reality of Genesis, our view of ourselves will never be the same. No longer will we experience our lives and our pain as either meaningless or insignificant. The understanding that there exists beyond ourselves, beyond our limited everyday consciousness, a source of power and strength that nourishes our very being changes us forever. We become true co-creators of our realities, guided by an invisible presence of unimaginable wisdom, strength, and compassion. With this perspective, with this feeling with this lifestyle, we can traverse the universe with infinitely more clarity than our limited and unaided consciousness is capable.

We have shared with you our views, knowing that what is truly important is your view. Our words may have triggered thoughts, may have reminded you of some powerful early spiritual experiences, evoked feelings, or challenged you.

To paraphrase Milton Erickson (1980):

Into each life some confusion should come . . .
    also some enlightenment.
And may our words go with you
    and become the sound of the wind,
        the rain, the fire,
        the voice of your teachers
        and your friends
            and the beginning of a
            lifelong dialogue.

References

AA Grapevine. Dec., 1957. Quoted in **Came to Believe** . . . New York, N.Y., 1973.

AA World Services, Inc., **Pass it On,** New York. N.Y., 1984.

AA World Services, Inc., **Came to Believe** . . ., New York, N.Y., 1973.

Alcoholics, Learning Pub., Inc., Holmes Beach, FL, 1985.

American Heritage Dictionary, 2nd College edition. Dell Publishing Co. Inc., New York, N.Y., 1985.

Barnabei, Fred, Personal Communication, Phoenix, AZ, 1982.

Bhagavad Gita, Translated by Eknath Easwaran, Nilgiri Press, Petaluma, CA., 1985.

Black, Claudia, **It Will Never Happen to Me,** A.C.T., Denver, CO., 1981.

Black, Claudia, Conference Presentation, San Francisco, CA., 1985.

Black, Claudia, Conference Presentation, Washington, D.C., 1986.

Bodo, Murray, **Francis: The Journey and the Dream**, St. Anthony Messenger Press, Cincinnati, Ohio, 1972.

Booth, Fr. Leo., **Walking on Water**, Health Communications, Inc., Pompano Beach, FL, 1985.

Branden, Nathaniel, **The Disowned Self**, Bantam Books, New York, N.Y., 1971.

Campbell, Joseph, **The Hero's Journey**, A Mythology Limited Production, La Jolla, CA., 1986.

Cermak, T.L., U.S. Journal Presentation, Washington, D.C., 1986.

Cermak, T.L., **Diagnosing and Training Co-Dependence**, Johnson Institute Books, Minneapolis, MN, 1986.

Cermak, T.L., & Brown, S., "Group Therapy With the Adult Children of Alcoholics," *International Journal of Group Psychotherapy,* 32(3), 1982, 375-389.

A Course in Miracles, Foundation for Inner Peace, Farmingdale, N.Y., 1975.

Da Free, John, **Four Fundamental Questions**, Dawn Horse Press, Clearlake, CA, 1978.

Easwaran, Eknath, **Love Never Faileth**, Nilgiri Press, Petaluma, CA,. 1984.

Eliot, T.S., **Collected Poems**, Harcourt, Brace, World, New York, N.Y., 1963.

Ferguson, Marilyn, **Aquarian Conspiracy**, J.P. Tarcher, Inc., Los Angeles, CA., 1980.

Fishel, Ruth, **The Journey Within: A Spiritual Path To Recovery**, Health Communications, Pompano Beach, FL, 1987.

Fromm, Erick, **The Art of Loving**, Harper & Row, New York, N.Y., 1974.

Gandhi, Mohandas K., **An Autobiography: The Story of My Experiments With Truth**, Beacon Press, Boston, MA., 1957.

Goethe, Clavigo, **In His Works**, Robertson, Ashford & Bentley, London, 1902.

Gravitz, H.L., & Bowden, J.D., **Guide To Recovery: A Book for Adult Children of Alcoholics**, Learning Pub., Inc., Holmes Beach, FL, 1985.

Gravitz, H.L., & Bowden, J.D., **Recovery: A Guide for Adult Children of Alcoholics**, Simon & Schuster, Inc., New York, N.Y., 1987.

Greenleaf, Jael, Conference Presentation, San Francisco, CA., 1985.

Hari Dass, Baba, Personal Communication, Mt. Madonna, Watsonville, CA., Jan. 1986.

Hawthorne, Nathaniel, **The House of the Seven Gables**, Dodd, Mead & Co., Inc., New York, N.Y., 1950.

Holy Bible, Melton Book Co., Dallas, TX., 1971.

James, William, **The Varieties of Religious Experience**, Penguin, New York, N.Y., 1982.

Jampolsky, Gerald, **Love is Letting Go of Fear**, Bantam Books, Toronto, 1979.

Jampolsky, Gerald, **Teach Only Love**, Bantam Books, N.Y., 1983.

Jampolsky, Gerald, UC Ext. Workshop, Morrow Bay, CA., 1984.

Jampolsky, Gerald, UC Ext. Workshop, Santa Barbara, CA., Feb. 1, 1986.

Jones, E. Stanley, **Unshakable Kingdom, Unchanging Person**, Abingdon Press, New York, N.Y., 1979.

Joy, WB, **Joy's Way**, J.P. Tarcher Inc., Los Angeles, CA., 1979.

Jung, Carl G., **Memories, Dreams and Reflections**, Jaffe ed., Trans. Winston, Vintage, Random House, New York, N.Y., 1965.

Kazantzakas, Nikos, **St. Francis**, Simon & Schuster, Inc., New York, N.Y., 1965.

Keller, Carole, **Faith to Heal**, Unpublished Manuscript, Denver, CO., 1987.

Keyes, Ken. Jr., **The Hundredth Monkey**, Vision Books, Coos Bay, OR., 1982.

Kriyananda, Swami, **The Path: Autobiography of a Western Yogi**, Ananda Pub., Nevada City, CA., 1979.

Kurtz, Ernest, University of Chicago, **Not-God: A History of Alcoholics Anonymous**, Hazelden Educational Services, Center City, MN., 1979.

Leonard, George, **The Silent Pulse**, Delacorte Press, N.Y.,

1969.

Yogi Maharishi Mahesh, The Science of Being and Art of Living, International SRM Pub., Los Angeles, CA., 1963.

MacLaine, Shirley, Out on a Limb, Bantam Books, New York, N.Y., 1983.

Mandino, Og, The Greatest Salesman in the World, Bantam Books, New York, N.Y., 1968.

Maslow, Abraham, Toward a Psychology of Being, Van Nostrand, Princeton, N.J., 1962.

Maslow, Abraham, The Farther Reaches of Human Nature, Viking, New York, N.Y., 1971.

Millman, Dan, Personal communication, San Rafael, CA., June, 1987.

Muktananda, Swami, Where Are You Going? A Guide to the Spiritual Journey, Gurudev Siddah Peethm, Ganespuri, India, 1981.

Peck, M. Scott. The Road Less Traveled, Simon & Schuster, Inc., New York, N.Y., 1978.

Prabavananda, Swami, The Sermon on the Mount According to Vedanta, New American Library, New York, N.Y., 1963.

Rogers, Carl, "Reactions to Gunnison's Article on the Similarities Between Erickson, and Rogers". J. of Counseling and Dev., Vol. 63, May 1985. pp 565-66.

Rogers, John. "There is No Hurt," International Journal For Philosophy Of Religion. Vol. No. 3. 1985. pp 84-92.

Satir, Virginia, Conference Presentation, Los Angeles, CA., 1986.

Smith, Lillian, Quoted in Sermon by Rev. Tony Perino, Sept., 1981.

Spalding, Laird T. Life and Teaching of the Masters of the Far East, Vol. 1, De Vorss & Co., Marina Del Rey, CA., 1924.

Tamiazzo, John, Love and Be Loved, Newastle Pub., Inc., No. Hollywood, CA., 1986.

Tart, C.W., States of Consciousness, Dutton, New York, N.Y., 1975.

The Collected Works, Teresa of Avila, Rodrigues &

Kavanaugh, Institute of Carmelite Studies, Washington, 1980.

Thomsen, Robert, **Bill W.**, Harper & Row, New York, N.Y., 1975.

The Upanishads, Translated by F. Max Muller. Dover Publications, New York, N.Y., 1962.

Wayman, Rev. Dennis, Personal Communication, Santa Barbara, CA., June. 1985, April, 1986.

Wegscheider-Cruse, Sharon, **Choicemaking,** Health Communications, Inc., Pompano Beach, FL, 1985.

White Eagle, **Morning Light On The Spiritual Path,** White Eagle Pub., England, 1957.

Whitfield, C.L., **Alcoholism, Other Drug Problems, and Spirituality: Stress Management and Serenity During Recovery,** The Resource Group, Baltimore, MD., 1984.

Whitfield, C.L., **Healing the Child Within: Discovery and Recovery for Adult Children.** Health Communications, Pompano Beach, FL., 1986.

Whitfield, C.L., Personal Communication, Santa Barbara, CA., 1986.

Wilcove, R.N., Personal Communication, Santa Barbara, CA., 1986.

Yogananda, Paramahansa, **Autobiography Of A Yogi,** SRF Pub., Los Angeles, CA., 1946.

Yogananda, Paramahansa, **Self-Realization Fellowship Lessons,** SRF Pub., Los Angeles, CA., 1956.